"Mick's story will resonate with those who, lik
tribute to the protection and care of vulnerable
may not take on a national system of care, as
something to encourage the care for children i

—ELLI OSWALD
Interim Executive Director, Faith to Action Initiative

"Wrapped within a humorous and personal narrative, this book contains a powerful illustration of how one man with a true passion for justice can create a ripple effect, reaching from the gutters of favelas to the offices of influential government agencies. Anyone who cares about children should read it."

—HELEN CONWAY
District Judge

"Learning from their own mistakes, this book shows that families are the best place for children to be raised. Professional skills are needed to ensure that children's needs are met. As Mick asks, 'Would you want your own child to be cared for in an orphanage?' If not, why is this good enough for other children?"

—RUTH BARLEY
Sheffield Hallam University, UK

"From the coal mines of Yorkshire, to the favelas of Brazil, to the intolerable orphanages of Romania and Tajikistan, to the villages of Myanmar, this book will take you around the world as it follows a man with only one goal in his heart—the well-being of the world's vulnerable children. This book raises vital and urgent questions about orphanages and children's villages; it offers many practical examples of alternative forms of care. I commend it you warmly."

—KRISH KANDIAH
Founding Director of Home for Good

"Children flourish in families. I hope the inspirational account in this highly readable book encourages many more families from across the world to come forward to care for children who would previously have never experienced the love and joy which family life can uniquely provide."

—FIONA BRUCE
Member of Parliament

Children Belong in
Families

Children Belong in
Families

A Remarkable Journey
Towards Global Change

Mick Pease and Philip Williams

Foreword by Baroness Caroline Cox

RESOURCE *Publications* · Eugene, Oregon

Resource Publications
An Imprint of Wipf and Stock Publishers
199 W. 8th Ave., Suite 3
Eugene, OR 97401

www.wipfandstock.com

PAPERBACK ISBN: 978-1-5326-4433-7
HARDCOVER ISBN: 978-1-5326-4434-4
EBOOK ISBN: 978-1-5326-4435-1

Manufactured in the U.S.A.   11/05/18

Some names and identifying details have been changed to protect the privacy of individuals.

Back Cover Illustration: Drawn by a Brazilian child to show the contrast between his home—bright and cheerful—and the institution where he was sent, dark and forbidding.

To
the family where I belong,
George (1923–1996), Ada (1926–2000), Brenda, Mark, and Kevin.

Contents

Foreword

I AM DELIGHTED TO provide this foreword to an account of the journey of Mick and Brenda Pease. They have run their remarkable UK-registered child protection charity with passion and dedication over the last two decades and told me several times how our unexpected encounter in Brazil provided the catalyst for all that followed. If my advice during that brief lunchtime conversation triggered so much, I count it a privilege to have played a part. Over twenty years ago Mick and Brenda were virtually lone voices in what has now become a global movement to support safe, family-based care for abandoned or vulnerable children. I am thrilled to see the values they embody spreading across other organizations and helping to shape practice and policies around the world.

When Mick first set up his charity he called it Substitute Families for Abandoned Children (SFAC). I am pleased to hear that it is now *Strengthening* Families for Abandoned Children. The subtle change of name reflects development toward capacity-building for families, communities, and organizations. Family-based care can flourish in all communities with encouragement and support. SFAC and like-minded individuals and organizations provide that training and support. It need not stop there. These developments can be transmitted and passed on.

My own work previously through Christian Solidarity International (CSI) and now with the Humanitarian Aid Relief Trust (HART) has touched on the kind of areas that SFAC address. When I visited the Soviet Union in 1989 and 1990 I saw the shocking conditions endured by children in orphanages. At that time there were some 750,000 abandoned children across Russia. In St. Petersburg alone there were 19,000 children in special institutions and another 10,000 who were homeless. Perhaps the most shocking statistic of all was that only 6 percent of children in institutions were fully orphaned, without either parent. The others had been abandoned.[1]

One of the first humanitarian initiatives we undertook through CSI was a return visit to Russia with a team of psychologists and pediatricians. Our reports and recommendations were hard-hitting but nevertheless well received. They helped to pave the way for extensive reforms as the Soviet Union gave way to the Russian Federation.[2]

There are other parallels between my work and Mick and Brenda's. I have lobbied in the UK House of Lords on behalf of oppressed minorities or those caught up in "forgotten conflicts" such as in the Armenian enclave of Nagorno-Karabakh, in the jungles of Myanmar, and in war-torn Sudan.

Mick and his team speak for the voiceless, in their case, abandoned children with no say or influence on the care or support they receive. They demonstrate how family-based solutions, foster care, kinship care, and other forms of relational care can and do work in even the most challenging settings.

All too often I have seen that well-meaning efforts are not always accompanied by sound professional practice. Not so with Mick and those with whom he works and whom he has influenced. The work of his charity and that of others with whom he collaborates is supported by solid research and sound practice. Passion will only get you so far. From the outset, Mick's enthusiasm was matched by the highest levels of professionalism and integrity. Mick is able to inspire others and, equally importantly, set measures and procedures in place to ensure compliance with professional standards.

To read Mick and Brenda's story is to discover how ordinary people can do extraordinary things. It is a story of grit and determination to keep going against the odds. The challenge is enormous: some 150 million children around the world do not live with their natural families. The shocking reality is that this is preventable. Many children in residential care have one or other parent living or close relatives who could care for them. As the tide continues to turn toward family-based care as an alternative to residential solutions, there is an urgent need for training, information, and support. The initial impetus came through UNICEF, Save the Children, and other international charities and non-governmental organizations (NGOs). Today it is a global grassroots movement. Mick was an early pioneer of this

1 . Cox, *Trajectories of Despair*, 8.
2 . Boyd, *A Voice for the Voiceless*, 94–113.

movement and SFAC has provided training, advice and support in some thirty countries. Mick works with people of all faiths and none, just as I have in my humanitarian and advocacy work. He works with both secular and faith-based aid and development agencies, with government social services and the judiciary.

The principles he works with are universal, the challenges global. Mick is motivated by his strong Christian faith, but his work crosses boundaries of creed and culture. He is not promoting a Western approach but a relational one that can be adapted for very different societies, cultures, and circumstances. It is a holistic vision and an integrated approach. It takes account of indigenous cultures and the features of particular societies. Most importantly of all, it focuses on the needs of the child. This has always been center stage in the work of SFAC. In Mick's words, "our work is never about us, our faith, our organization, it is always about the child who should be at the center of everything we do."

I am delighted to hear how, in the UK, the US, Australia, and elsewhere, Christian churches and denominations have adjusted their approach to childcare and child protection. In Africa there are indigenous movements and initiatives with similar aims. They work with churches, community groups, elders, and tribal leaders to find, support, and strengthen safe family-based homes for abandoned children.

Sadly, in some parts of the world inappropriate residential care is part of the problem. Christian, other faith-based, and secular organizations have all done very important work, but some perpetuate the issues SFAC seeks to redress. Children in residential care can become institutionalized, cut off from their cultures and communities, isolated from their ethnic origins and heritage. Evidence shows that children are happier, perform better educationally, and flourish in secure and safe families. It sounds so obvious, but it needs to be said. *Children belong in families.*

It is important for our societies and vitally important to each child. Thanks to the work of organizations like SFAC, this is increasingly becoming a possibility for abandoned children in many parts of the world. The rest of us can help by aligning ourselves with that ethos and vision, as individuals, as organizations, and as societies. As you read this account, I hope you will be encouraged, inspired, and informed and, however you can, support their work and promote their vision.

Baroness Cox

Acknowledgments

"MICK, HAVE YOU EVER thought about writing a book about all this?"

I've lost count of the number of times I've heard that question. If you've ever asked it, thanks for prompting me. If you haven't, I hope you'll read on and understand why it was asked!

I'm grateful to everyone who has helped bring this book into being.

To Wipf & Stock, especially Matthew Wimer and his team for all their help.

To Phil Williams whose unexpected text triggered the process as I awaited yet another flight and who followed it through. To Natalie Watson for her advice on pitching and publishing. To Jon Wilcox for his diligent copyediting and unexpected knowledge of Burmese traditions! To so many others for their patience and encouragement.

More broadly, I'd like to thank Tony and Vivienne Hodges and other supporters. Without their faithful support, SFAC could not have strengthened so many families and improved the lives of thousands of children worldwide. I thank my parents for coping with me and Brenda for holding on to me. She is my constant anchor and support. I commend Mark and Kevin for finding their own families and following their own calls.

Thank you to everyone who caught our passion and the values we hold. Thank you for trusting and believing in us.

1. The Mystery Man and the Baroness

"YOU HAVE FIVE DAYS to leave the country."

My Portuguese may not have been the best, but I understood that much. I felt the impact even more when the federal guard scribbled in my passport and pressed the rubber stamp home. Bam! One curt comment, a single jab, and our plans were squashed, our work at an end.

Brenda and I were working at a Brazilian children's home on tourist visas. We had visited friends in Paraguay and were crossing the border on our return. Like many others, we had seen TV coverage and read news reports of the murders of street children. Restaurant owners, hoteliers, and shopkeepers were hiring armed men to rid the streets of nuisance home-less kids. They called them "the disposable ones." Off-duty security guards, policemen even, were paid to execute these kids by night. Bang! A bullet in the back of the head, the body dumped on waste ground. No ID, no birth certificate or documents. No name.

These reports shocked the world. They shocked us too. We had to do something. Our two boys had grown up. Mark was studying and Kevin developing a plumbing business. We now had the time and opportunity to try and make a difference. I took a year's leave of absence from my job as a social worker with Leeds City Council in the north of England. Brenda left her administrative job and we set off. The boys moved into the house and we put everything on hold.

Here we were, six months in, and the whole thing had suddenly col-lapsed. We were gutted. "Don't worry," everyone told us. "This is Brazil. They are so laid-back here. All you have to do after three months is ask the federal police whether you can stay longer. Then, after six months, you can cross the border to Bolivia or Paraguay and come back again. It's a formality, a quick stamp on your passport and the visa is extended. Everyone does it, missionaries, aid workers. It's no big deal, no paperwork, no fuss, no questions asked."

Yes, this was Brazil, but this time, questions were asked. What did we think we were doing, crossing into Paraguay and then back again?

"We have been visiting friends."

We genuinely had. We stayed a week with friends in the capital Asunción, unlike some aid workers on tourist visas who simply crossed the border, turned around, and walked back into Brazil.

We had crossed the border at Foz do Iguaçu where the conurbation extends as Cuidad del Este on the Paraguayan side and traveled onward by bus to the capital. Now we were stopped at the checkpoint as we tried to return.

"You can't do this," said the federal guard. "You cannot renew. You have five days to leave the country." Stamp.

We exchanged very few words as the coach rumbled through the night and all the next day toward São Paulo. For twenty hours the vast Brazilian landscape rolled by; hills, plains, cities and settlements, pockets of forest. We were in no mood to enjoy the views, no mood even to talk. We had to leave Brazil and had no idea what we would do next. We both felt stunned, let down, abandoned, and alone.

The staff at the missionary organization we worked with were not at all perturbed.

"Don't worry," they said, "This is Brazil. We have contacts, we can put in a word for you. It'll soon be sorted out. Leave it with us, we'll go into the city and speak to the authorities."

Days passed and no word came. We carried on as if in a daze, caring for the kids we'd come to know and love. We played games with the older children and washed and fed the younger ones. We gave them a structure and routine to establish the secure boundaries children need. Most were just ordinary kids. What they lacked was personal attention; a family atmosphere and environment. We loved those kids. I had spent weeks repainting the rusty old climbing frame in the play area. We both spent hours with Matheus, a toddler with hydrocephalus. We talked to him in his cot and pulled faces to make him laugh. Every day we took him out of his cot to learn to walk. Eventually, he reached the children's playground and climbing frame, gurgling and chuckling with delight. It was this kind of interaction and personal connection that made it all so worthwhile.

People often talk about a "calling," a sense of vocation. Brenda and I had felt it since we first met but had no idea at that time how this would work out. She was a farmer's daughter from Devon in the rural southwest of England. I was a Yorkshire coal miner from the industrial north. I left school with no qualifications and no prospects. I had no interest in learning or education. We both came from devout Christian families and met at an annual preaching convention in Filey on the Yorkshire coast. It was there that I sensed some kind of "call," an impression that I wanted to do something more than simply earn a living, something that could make a difference. From our particular church backgrounds, the expectation was that this would involve missionary work or church leadership. Neither of us had any desire to do such things. All we knew was that we wanted to do *something*. On the strength of this vague impression, we left our mining village and enrolled at a Bible college in the English Midlands. We had no prior academic qualifications and no idea what we were going to do afterward.

After Bible college we worked for three years as houseparents in a children's home. From there I would go on to qualify as a social worker, specializing in child protection, adoption, and fostering.[1] Gradually we began to develop a clearer idea of what the "calling" might involve; something involving children and families.

So here we were, in Brazil, fulfilling what we then believed to be the outcome of that "call." Hands-on intervention. Working with street kids in a rescue mission. It all seemed to fit our expectations. Suddenly it was all coming to an end.

We had come to a Christian missionary complex in São Paulo State. I had been to Brazil before, initially to Belo Horizonte in 1994 at the invitation of YWAM (Youth With A Mission), a short-term mission agency that

1. Fostering and adoption practice inevitably varies from country to country. For example, fostering and adoption are increasingly seen in the US as a continuum and, according to a recent UK government review, 40% of the approximately 135,000 adoptions in the US each year start as fostering placements (Narey and Owers, *Foster Care*, 96). In contrast, very few fostering placements in England convert to adoption. According to government statistics, as of March 2017 there were 72,670 children in care in England, 74% of which were in fostering placements (UK Government, *Children*, 8). In 2017, 4,350 children in care were adopted, falling 8% from 2016 (Ibid., 13). A high proportion (86%) of children adopted were under three years old (Ibid., 14). Figures for Scotland, Wales, and Northern Ireland are recorded separately.

was developing an interest in issues around adoption. They wanted me to tell them more about it, how it worked in the UK, how it might be developed in Brazil. I returned the following year, imparting more information, meeting missionaries and social workers. On those occasions, I visited during my normal vacation allocation from Leeds City Council. Then, in 1997, impelled by the news of street shootings and murders, Brenda and I both came intending to stay for a year, unpaid, to try to make a difference.

We had written to some twenty-five missionary or development agencies offering our services. We wrote to all the Christian charities we could find which offered some kind of child or family care. The response opened my eyes. Most replied, but in each case, the response was broadly the same. What could they possibly do with a social worker? I wish we had kept those letters. A quarter of a century on they would appear even more outrageous than they did at the time.

What were they telling us?

If you are a car mechanic, we could use you in the mission field. If you are in primary health care or are an engineer, we could use you in the mission field. If you are an expert in agriculture or irrigation, a bricklayer and can build, a teacher and can teach English—we could use you in the mission field. But a *social worker?*

Yet every one of these organizations had some form of work with children or families. That was the very reason we had approached them. What did this mean? That if you were any Tom, Dick, and Harry you could work with kids? That if you were a social worker they wouldn't know what to do with you? A bricklayer or a car mechanic, then yes, we can use your skills. We deliver health care so we could certainly use a nurse—but a social worker? You don't have to be a social worker or have any qualifications or experience to work with kids.

I found this massively insulting, but quite apart from the affront to my professional dignity, there were more serious implications. What did this say about the level of professionalism involved? It struck me then and it stays with me now. I realized that many of the people working with children through mission, aid, or development agencies were doing so with good intentions but without the practical or professional skills required. They were working from the heart, but with no real knowledge of how to respond to kids suffering from trauma or loss. The attitude seemed to be, "Right, you are a parent yourself. You understand kids." But there was no real insight that this in itself was not enough. These kids had particular problems. They were suffering from abuse and neglect. They needed specialist help. Something had to change.

It was the day before we were due to fly back to the UK. The leaders of the mission complex had made inquiries on our behalf.

"There's no more we can do," they told us. "You will have to fly back home. But you can always come back. Apply for missionary visas, come back and join us . . ."

I lent dejectedly on the metal windowsill of one of the bare, simple office rooms and gazed out over the dusty parking lot. A man in a white shirt was walking across it. He didn't look Latin American, but that was not at all unusual for multicultural Brazil, particularly within a missionary complex with regular visitors from around the world. What was unusual was how, when he looked up and saw me, he addressed me in a British accent.

"You alright?"

"Not really," I sighed, my dejection blunting the surprise at hearing a familiar accent. In many countries, including Brazil, people who could speak English often spoke it with an American tinge.

"Why?"

"It's a long story."

"Well, do you want to tell me about it?"

We spoke for a few minutes through the window then the stranger asked me to come down to talk further in the parking lot. I did so and I told him who we were, why I was feeling so downcast, and asked him who he was.

"Does it matter who I am?" he said enigmatically. "I want to hear your story."

We spoke for a long time, maybe up to an hour. I told him how we had come to work with street kids and how our plans had come to an abrupt end. He must have sensed my irritation and frustration. It was clear he understood it, but he also encouraged me to consider the wider context, to put things in perspective. So many aid workers or missionaries came in thinking they had all the answers. They tried to impose solutions from outside. Instead, they should work alongside and in step with the cultures and societies of the host countries themselves. This was their country, their history, their culture.

After a while, he stopped me and said, "I don't know why I am listening to you, but I feel a prompting—and I believe it is from God—to hear you out some more. I'm busy right now, but I would like to invite you and your wife to my apartment this evening. We can speak for an hour perhaps. Seven o'clock?"

I accepted his offer. We knew the area where he was staying, accommodation for visitors and for missionaries who had bought land and built houses for themselves. I went to tell Brenda, realizing as I did so that I did not know his name.

We turned up at the mystery man's apartment at seven o'clock as arranged. As evangelical Christians, we were familiar with prayers and "promptings." We also knew that there were visitors on-site and we had even heard talk of a delegation from the British government visiting our part of Brazil. We were intrigued. Who was this guy who had invited us around to talk?

"You can call me Sam," he said. "I work for Baroness Cox."

Baroness Cox? We had heard the name but knew little about her. We knew she had a peerage and sat in the House of Lords, the upper chamber of the UK Parliament. Beyond that, we knew nothing at that stage, although she was to become well known for her humanitarian work and advocacy in trouble spots around the world.[2] She was in Brazil to receive an award from the government in recognition of her work.

"So, what do you do back home?" Sam asked.

"I am an adoption and fostering social worker."

"And what do you do as an adoption and fostering social worker? What does it involve?"

"Well, I investigate and assess if children are safe where they live. I've been a residential social worker and seen how it works in the UK. Here in Brazil, I've seen that a lot of the kids in care are there not because they are bad kids, but because people have given up on them or because there's not been another option where they can live. In the UK we wouldn't place those kids into children's homes because it's not best for them. Instead we look for substitute families, either foster carers or adoptive parents. So why is it that here in Brazil they are hanging around in children's homes forever and a day and, in some cases, horrible ones at that? It's something I've observed since we've been here and I think there is another way."

---

2. Baroness Caroline Cox of Queensbury, born in 1937, is a crossbench member of the UK House of Lords. She received a life peerage in 1982 and was deputy speaker from 1985 to 2005. She is CEO of Humanitarian Aid Relief Trust and a patron of Christian Solidarity Worldwide, acting as its president until 2006. She is the subject of two biographies: Boyd, *A Voice for the Voiceless* and Gilbert, *Eyewitness to a Broken World*.

Sam listened then asked if we could pray. He said a short prayer asking that things would become clear for us and that we might have wisdom and strength to make the right decisions.

After he prayed, Sam looked up and asked, "You are leaving tomorrow?"

"Yes, in the afternoon. Our bags are packed and we are leaving for the airport after lunch. So, tomorrow morning we are going to say goodbye to the kids. We don't know whether we will be coming back."

"Baroness Cox and I are having lunch with the leaders of the mission in the refectory tomorrow," Sam said. "I'd like to invite you to join us. Then the van can take you to the airport."

The next day, we said goodbye to the kids. It was an emotional parting. We had grown very fond of them, particularly little Matheus and his sister, so brave and determined despite his condition. We pulled up outside the refectory in one of the mission vehicles. Leaving our luggage outside, we entered the long canteen to find the mission leaders, Sam, and the Baroness at one of the tables. She looked homely and very ordinary, not at all as we expected. It's not every day that a former miner and a farmer's daughter get to meet a Lord or Lady. They beckoned us over.

"How do I address a Baroness?" I asked as we were introduced.

"Just call me Caroline," she said with a reassuring smile.

We both sat alongside Lady Cox. "Sam has told me all about you," she said, "Now you tell me why you are here."

We told her our story over the next thirty minutes as we ate our lunch. I repeated the observations I'd made to Sam about the lack of fostering opportunities in Brazil. Once we had finished she said, "Now, here's what I think you should do. Go back and apply for a missionary visa and once you've got one come back here. But, Mick, don't work directly with the children as you have up until now. Instead, conduct some research into why fostering isn't happening in Brazil as it is in the UK and other countries. Once you have done that, you can see whether you can start to introduce foster care into Brazil."

My first thought was, "Me?"

Who was I to do this? I don't have any money. I don't have any contacts. I've never done this before. I don't know how to go about it.

I felt like Moses in the story of the burning bush when God called him to go back to Egypt to urge Pharaoh to release the Israelites from captivity.[3]

---

3. Exod 2–3.

What if they don't listen to me? Don't send me. I'm not eloquent. I can't speak that well.

"I'm telling you now," said Baroness Cox, "If foster care isn't happening in Brazil and if abandoned or homeless children can't go back to their families, there have to be ways to find alternatives. With your professional background and experience, you can help to identify what those might be."

So, we left the refectory and returned to the van for the drive to the airport. We did not see Baroness Cox again until she invited us to meet her at the House of Lords in 2017 although we maintained occasional contact by mail. I would meet Sam again later in equally intriguing circumstances.

All that lay ahead. For now, we flew back to the UK energized. Perhaps we hadn't got things completely wrong after all? The answer had been there in front of us and we hadn't noticed it. We had been doing the hands-on care, but really, we should look to influence things at a wider level. With my social work background and training, I could engage with other social workers, with academics and the judiciary, with policy makers and shapers.

We left the color and vibrancy of Brazil to return to a dank, dark English November. We moved back into our house where Mark and Kevin had been staying with a student friend. They weren't expecting us back so soon. Brenda was struck by the enormous bright yellow Homer Simpson poster on our living room wall that had replaced a reproduction of a classic painting!

We were part of a lively church in Leeds. They were very supportive and even took up a collection to pay for our return airfare. We explained what had happened, why our year in Brazil had been curtailed, and began to outline what we planned to do next.

I was buzzing with ideas about how to proceed. As Christmas approached I was so preoccupied I found I couldn't get into the spirit of it at all. Brenda could. She was pleased to be home. She had missed the lads and family and suffered ill-health for much of our time in Brazil. The accommodation was basic, the climate humid. At one point, she suffered horribly with a tropical intestinal worm until the Brazilian health services removed it. She was understandably relieved to be home. We had wondered whether our year in Brazil would lead to us living there longer term, working directly with street kids. Now we could see a way that was potentially more effective. With a missionary visa, I could return to carry out the research and advocacy work that Baroness Cox recommended. I could deploy my skills and expertise in a way we had not considered before. We had become too embroiled in meeting the immediate emergency needs. Now we could step back, take stock, and begin to address the broader issues. I now understood I had to work with those in positions of influence.

We left Brazil in late November 1997. By early February 1998, we were back. The intervening months were a whirlwind. We had been back and forth to the Brazilian embassy in London, sorting out visa requirements. I had to get the police checks done all over again, even though they had already been completed previously. I knew the procedures and how to lobby at the most senior levels to process the paperwork as soon as possible. There was no time to waste. We only had six months before my leave of absence expired and I returned to work.

During those last months in Brazil, I had meeting after meeting. I was now operating outside the faith sector, engaging secular agencies and authorities, judges, psychologists, and academics. I addressed groups of magistrates, senior officials, and administrators. People heard I was there talking about foster care as an alternative to institutional care. They came looking for me. They wanted to hear what I had to share. I am often asked how that came about. How an unknown social worker, a former miner from the north of England, found himself dealing with elected officials and senior authorities, initially in Brazil and then around the world? How did I get the introductions? Why did they want to listen to me in the first place?

I can only say that it happened and that it happened very quickly, far more quickly than the painfully slow process of implementation and change. There was an openness and candor among the Brazilian professionals and a fascination with the British fostering system. In England and Wales if it is considered unsafe for a child to remain at home, local government tries various measures to improve the situation. If nothing changes then the local authority applies for a court order to remove the child from parental care. An independent social worker and lawyer are appointed to ensure the child's views are central to any decisions made on their behalf. The judiciary is no longer involved once the court order is issued unless there is any need for further legal changes. The local government is responsible for all decisions, where a child lives, who they see and their overall welfare. In Brazil and some other countries there is a tendency for the judiciary to remain involved after issuing the order. They take active oversight of the care process and a child may not be fostered without their consent.

The Brazilian legal system differs from that of English-speaking countries. If I were to stand any chance at all of influencing policies and practice, I had to reach the judiciary. I had to find a platform. I had to earn the right to be heard. I had to understand the system if I was to help influence change.

My main contacts during my previous visits were with missionary organizations. They had dealings and contacts with the authorities of course, but the connections I now made happened independently. The most significant of these were with Isa Guará and her colleague Maria Lucia in São Paulo. Isa held a senior position in the city's social services working with older children. Maria was a child psychologist and research academic. They invited me around to Maria's home at ten on a Saturday morning, so I beat my way there by bus through the bustle of the sprawling city. We were there the rest of the day, talking excitedly well into the evening. Both women could speak some English and could understand far more and between that and my very basic Portuguese we were able to communicate.

"Tell us about the English system," they said. "We want to know all about it."

I explained that it was not my intention to promote or recommend a British approach over any other. Our system was far from perfect but it was consistent and there were aspects they might find helpful. For all its flaws, the British system was based on the premise that children belong in families, not institutions. The UK, along with most North American and European countries, had moved away from institutional solutions in favor of family-based care. All the evidence showed that children placed with foster families or with adoptive parents, irrespective of economic circumstances, fared better socially and educationally than those brought up in institutions.[4]

I related how I had worked in the residential care system and knew it from the inside. My role as a social worker was to find safe and secure

4. The detrimental effects of large-scale institutional care on child development have been documented since the early twentieth century. The American behavioral scientist Henry Dwight Chapin used statistical procedures to chart critical periods of social development across institutionalized infants at a time when the mortality rate in some US orphanages approached 100 percent (Gray, "Henry Dwight Chapin"). John Bowlby and many others reached similar conclusions in the mid-twentieth century. More recently, in 2007, the Bucharest Early Intervention Project compared the developmental capacities of children raised in large institutions with those in families and foster care. The study found shocking evidence of impaired physical development as well as lower IQ and higher rates of social and behavioral abnormalities (Nelson et al., "Caring").

family-based care for children unable to live with their family, either with foster parents or through adoption. I told them how I would arrange background and safeguarding checks, how the legal requirements operated, what support and training were available for foster parents.

I told them what I had observed of social work education and training in Brazil. There was nothing I could add on the academic and theoretical side. Brazil has universities that rank among the best in the world[5] and Universidade de São Paulo is reckoned to be the best in Ibero-America.[6]

Social work education in Brazil was stimulating and academically rigorous yet often with little scope for students to gain practical experience. As a child psychologist, Maria knew all the accepted and standard texts and theories used the world over. The pioneering work on attachment theory by John Bowlby,[7] later work by American and Australian practitioners—none of this was new in Brazil. The issue was not the quality of social work education but the lack of opportunity for application.

Competition for places at the higher quality, publicly funded universities is intense. A third of Brazilian graduates study at private or for-profit institutions. These run courses during the evenings as well as daytime so that people can work and study at the same time. It is common for a Brazilian student to work from 7:30 a.m. to around 6 p.m. and then spend from 7 p.m. to 11 p.m. in lectures and tutorials. There are few opportunities for practical fieldwork in disciplines like psychology and social care. Students work to support themselves unless their parents can afford to do so and this limits the opportunity for practical placements and hands-on training.

---

5. See the QS BRICS University Rankings 2018 at https://www.topuniversities.com/.

6. The university has featured among the top hundred worldwide in various league tables, University Ranking by Academic Performance (URAP), and the Times Higher Education and QS World Ranking tables.

7. John Bowlby (1907–90) was a British psychologist best known for his pioneering research into child development and issues of attachment and loss. He was born into an upper-middle-class family and, like many from that background at that time, was largely raised by a nanny and sent away to boarding school. He had little interaction with his mother when growing up. During the Second World War he carried out significant studies on children separated from their parents which led to his later groundbreaking development of attachment theory. Bowlby's research explored how children become attached to significant carers or "parental figures" when separated from their birth parents. His findings laid the foundations for later research and childcare practice. His best-known works are *Child Care and the Growth of Love* (1965) and *Attachment and Loss*, vols. 1 (1969), 2 (1973), and 3 (1980).

Fostering was virtually unknown in Brazil at that time. Isa and Maria were keen to hear my experience of it in the UK context. Adoption was better known but associated by many with international adoption by wealthy foreign couples. The situation was complex; so many barriers, so many obstacles. I had a lot to say yet Isa and Maria Lucia heard me out. I was in full flow when Isa Guará leaned forward and held up her hand.

"Mick," she said. "This can work in Brazil!"

2. Home

THEN IF SHE DIES, AT LEAST SHE'LL DIE AT HOME.

MATCHES, FIRE, SMOKE. BY the time Mrs. Gardner reached her kitchen, the whole thing was alight. They knew something was wrong when I dashed into the lounge and dived under the table where the television had pride of place. The table was covered by a cloth so I cowered beneath it.

"Hey up,"[1] they must have thought. "What's he done now?"

Only set fire to the kitchen, that's what. Mam had taken me around to Billy Gardner's house. I must have been about six or seven. While she was talking to his mother, I went into the kitchen with one or other of his brothers and sisters. There I found something I loved to play with, a box of matches. What's more, something to ignite, dishcloths hanging up to dry on a rack that stretched across the kitchen. Within seconds the room was full of choking smoke.

Mrs. Gardner soon put the fire out, but it could have been a lot worse. As a boy, I was forever getting into scrapes. I loved playing outside, soccer, cricket, throwing stones—particularly throwing stones. My father was a bricklayer. He always kept a stock of window panes handy to replace those I had broken or been suspected of breaking. "Who's broken that window? It must have been that Mick Pease . . ." Rather than pay for the damage, my father kept panes he had picked up from work. I hadn't always broken them, but I got the blame.

My mother caught me once throwing stones against the wall of our house.

"What are you doing?"

1. A common expression in the north of England, it can be used as a greeting or as a way of drawing attention to something.

13

"Throwing stones up again' a-wall . . ."

"But there's a window up there, you're going to hit it."

"No, I won't, I'm just trying to see how close I can get without hitting it."

My mother was furious, "You dare do that again!"

"Alright, I will," so I threw another.

"Right, you get yourself in here!"

"Why? I only did what you said, 'Dare do that again . . .'"

Of course, I knew very well what she meant. I chose to interpret it differently. In training and advocacy, I use this incident to reinforce a serious point. When we deal with issues affecting children's lives we must choose our words carefully and be absolutely clear in what we say and how we say it.

I was an energetic lad. I was always playing in the street, in neighbors' houses, and I liked to talk. Boy, could I talk! Nobody would tell me anything in case I spread it around. We were the last family in our street to get a TV set. I was cock-a-hoop to find out we were getting one at last only to learn that the whole neighborhood knew about it already.

I asked Mam and Dad, "How come everyone else knew we were getting a telly and I didn't?"

"If we'd told you, it would be all around t'town by now."

"But you didn't tell me and it's still all around t'town!"[2]

Many of my childhood experiences informed my later work. I grew up on a council estate in the north of England, what would be termed a public housing project in the United States. The houses were all built between the wars. They represented an improvement on the Victorian and Edwardian terraced houses and back-to-backs where most industrial workers lived.

It was a rough, tough place but with a strong sense of community. People looked out for each other, cared for one another. Whenever money was tight, as it often was, they would borrow a cup of rice or sugar, or a few shillings from neighbors and friends to buy food until the next payday. It was a close-knit, white working-class, blue-collar community. There was

---

2. One of the most distinctive features of northern English speech is the habit of reducing or not pronouncing the definite article "the." Instead, it is replaced by an abbreviated "t" sound, produced simultaneously with a glottal stop. In some cases, there is barely any discernible sound there at all and it appears to outsiders that the definite article is missing entirely. English readers from outside the UK may be familiar with it from the novels of Emily Brontë and D. H. Lawrence.

high unemployment. Those in work earned low wages through manual labor. There were problems with drink and domestic violence. Gangs of lads would intimidate youth from other areas who dared to come onto our estate. It was largely low-level violence, pushing someone off their bike, a quick scuffle with fists. Sometimes it got more serious, as my teenage sister was to find out.

Despite all this, it was a great place to grow up in many ways. In those days, even in cold, wet northern England, people would spend more time outdoors, chatting to their neighbors. As I go around the world, I encounter both rural and large urban communities which are still like that, very much like British society in the 1950s. People chat with one another across a yard or over a garden fence just as we did in my mining community back then. There are kinship structures and community links that play a very positive role in the work we now do with vulnerable and abandoned children.

Although we had a strong sense of community, it was also a very deferential society. People knew their place. It was drummed into us in school, in the factories, mills, and mines. We had low expectations and adhered to unwritten rules and codes. Certain things went unmentioned or were whispered behind closed doors. A teenage girl might disappear for a while only to turn up several months later. They had been "staying with an aunt." They had been ill, had problems of some kind, had to go away. We were never told why. Only later did we realize that they were pregnant. They were sent away to avoid shame on the family. British society has become far more liberal since then, of course, but we encounter these attitudes today too in our work around the world. People are marginalized or outcast because they are thought to have brought shame or dishonor on their families and communities. People are isolated because they are different or because they don't conform.

Where I grew up, outsiders were rare. Someone from a neighboring town or village would attract attention. It was even more uncommon to see someone of a different race or ethnicity. I can remember the first time I saw a black person. A woman near us was rumored to be dating a black man. I must have been about seven or eight years old and remember waiting near her house with my friends. We had to see for ourselves. Now I know what it is like to go into regions where I might be the first white person people have seen. They want to hold my hand and touch my skin to see if it is different to theirs. Every stranger can become a neighbor. What is familiar to us is unfamiliar to someone else. Our work is all about context, contact, communication, community.

Knottingley was a grim industrial town on the River Aire in Yorkshire, England's largest county. The southern and western parts of Yorkshire were industrial powerhouses—coal, steel, textiles. To enter the north of the county was to enter another world, to experience the stunningly scenic Yorkshire Dales and Moors. Once a thriving inland port, Knottingley was still an important center for boat-building and glass and chemical works. It was close to what became the UK's last working deep coal mine, Kellingley Colliery, where I had my first job.[3] The three cooling towers at nearby Ferrybridge power station were the tallest in Europe and could be seen all over the county. This was the industrial north at its grimiest and most Dickensian—smoke, soot, grit. Small wonder the health authorities wanted to take my sister out of this environment when they found she had chronic asthma. Nothing could have prepared her, or my parents, for the impact this would have on our family.

George Pease met and married my mother, Ada Cassidy, during the Second World War. He was serving as a soldier and she worked in the NAAFI,[4] the organization that provided tea, toast, and cheer to British forces. George was one of two sons born to William and Alice Pease. William's mother died in childbirth and his father didn't have the necessary support both to work and care for a child. So my grandfather was sent some distance away to be bought up by his Aunt and Uncle Tasker. William never knew his father, nor whether he had other siblings, but retained the Pease family name. Alice's mother also died young. Her father remarried and because her stepmother didn't like Alice she sent her away to work as a domestic servant to another family.

My parents were Pentecostals and very devout. The Pentecostal movement started almost simultaneously on both sides of the Atlantic in the early 1900s. It featured fervent and lively worship, spiritual gifts, and a strong emphasis on prayer for healing. In the UK it grew and spread in working-class areas like ours.

To grow up Pentecostal was to inhabit a highly charged spiritual atmosphere and a life that largely revolved around church. My father was church

---

3. Kellingley Colliery opened in 1965 and closed in 2015. It was the last deep coal mine in Britain with shafts around half a mile deep.

4. Navy, Army and Air Force Institutes.

secretary and Sunday school superintendent. When he wasn't working he was doing something at the chapel. My mother, although no less fervent, used to complain at times that church always came first. In bad weather, he was unable to work and no work meant no pay. Even so, he would diligently set money aside for The Bible Society, for The Leprosy Mission, for church funds and missionary work around the world.

"We can't afford to keep ourselves," my mother would say. "Let's look to our own family first. The church can have its share later."

Yet he would carry on regardless, funding missions with his hard-earned "brass."[5]

I always knew we had little money and must have made things difficult for my parents with my relentless moans and requests for this and that. I couldn't understand why my father insisted on helping all these other people!

If the community I grew up in was close-knit and insular, the church culture reflected that too. Yet there was also an outward-looking aspect, a concern for others that went beyond our small, grimy town and into the world beyond. My father knew he would have little opportunity to travel, but he did what he could in the only way he knew. He gave money we could often ill afford to causes he believed in. He was a gentle, faithful, and diligent man. We were all thrilled when he later received the British Empire Medal for "services to industry."[6] My father eventually became clerk of works for our local government authority. It was his job to independently assess the quality of structural, mechanical, and engineering works. Nominations are made without the recipient knowing in advance. It was testimony to my father's hard work and attention to detail that architects and civic and community leaders all combined to put his name forward.

Mam was a very different character to Dad. She was sociable, friendly, and loved to talk about family, friends, and church. She took an interest in people. She never studied after leaving school and helped in the family bakery where she learned how to bake. I always remember listening to her sing as she baked and cooked. She often baked for people who were sick or going through difficult times. Mam had a strong sense of duty to her parents and siblings. Three of her brothers saw action in North Africa

5. A colloquial Yorkshire term for coins or currency in general.

6. The British Empire Medal, BEM, is awarded by the Queen for "hands-on service to the local community." For a list of UK honors, see UK Government, "Types of Honours and Awards."

during the Second World War. Her father was Irish and lost both legs in a mining accident. Little wonder the last place she wanted me to work was down the mines!

Churchgoing was more common in the UK in those days, even in poor working-class areas like ours. There were Anglicans and Methodists, the Salvation Army and Congregationalists. Even non-churchgoers sent their children to Sunday school, largely to give themselves a break. There were a lot of good folk involved with the churches and chapels even though the surrounding culture did not conform to their ideals. It took me a long time to realize that some of my "uncles" and "aunts" were not blood relatives at all. Rather, they were people my parents knew through church or were other neighbors and friends. We needed their support. I was eighteen months old when my sister Pamela was sent away to hospital on the coast.

When they got married my parents were told that they would not be able to have children. It was medically impossible. So they did what Pentecostals do. They devoted themselves to prayer. They called for the prayers of the elders of the church and of the congregation. During one prayer meeting, a minister prophesized that their prayers would be answered. They would most certainly bear children. Imagine their delight when Pamela was born in 1947. Imagine their anguish when they learned she had chronic asthma and was not expected to live.

I grew up without my sister at home. I was only aware I had one because of the photograph on the parlor wall. It showed a bonny toddler on the street outside our house, a pint of milk behind her on our doorstep.[7]

"Mam, Dad, who's that girl in the picture?"

"Your sister."

"Where is she? Why isn't she here?"

"She's away. She's ill."

Mam and Dad invariably changed the subject. Perhaps they wanted to spare me the pain they were going through. Around once a month, on a Saturday, my father would set off to visit her in the children's hospital near Liverpool. Sometimes my mother would go too. They could not always afford the fare for the two of them. I would be left with the Elleringtons, friends of my parents from church. I struck up a lifelong friendship with their son, John, who later became one of my charity's first trustees. We often got into scrapes and John sometimes hid in the outhouse with his ferret to

---

7. Most people had milk delivered in those days. The early morning British street scene was one of a bottle or two of milk on each front doorstep.

avoid Sunday school.[8] We were both rebels even then. Yes, we both continued with church and owned our parents' faith for ourselves, but we were not afraid to question or challenge anything we felt was ill thought through, unnecessary, or unhelpful.

It was the early 1950s and Britain's National Health Service (NHS) was still in its infancy. Founded in 1948, the NHS guaranteed treatment "free at the point of delivery" to everyone, irrespective of income, social level, or circumstances. It made, and still makes, an immense difference to people's lives, particularly those who are disadvantaged or on low incomes. Back then, however, officialdom and deference were still big factors in British society. What the man with the suit and tie or the nurse in the uniform said went unchallenged, even when the consequences were clearly less than ideal. The authorities said that Pamela had to be taken away to save her life and away she went. She was away from home for three Christmases, effectively four whole years.[9]

Officials told my parents that Pam would die unless she left our dirty, smoggy town. My parents had little choice. I'm told they could have faced criminal charges at that time if they didn't comply. We were poor. Where could we go? We didn't know anywhere else and our support networks were all very local. There seemed nothing for it but for my sister to go to that children's hospital on the coast to benefit from the bracing sea breeze.[10]

Astonishing as it may sound to us today, as late as the 1950s some children's respiratory hospitals still operated a drastic system recommended

8. British readers will associate such things with northern stereotypes, but people in the north of England often did keep ferrets, homing pigeons, and thin whippets, a dog rather like a small greyhound. The ferrets were pets but originally used for "rabbiting." The ferret would be sent down a warren to drive out rabbits which would be caught to augment the family diet.

9. Pamela's story appears in Morris and Priestley, *Journeys of Hope*, 125–36. Additional material from interviews by Philip Williams with Pamela and Brian Miller and with Mick Pease on December 5, 2017.

10. In the November 1919 issue of *British Medical Journal*, the UK's chief medical officer, T. Hartley Martin, wrote: "The treatment of surgical tuberculosis needs an open, barren, flat shore, exposed to the winds, with a fresh and equable temperature, moderate humidity and abundant sunshine . . . in the wards the majority of the children rapidly become accustomed to the open-air life, and although . . . the wards cannot be heated they [children] do not appear to feel the cold and make light of what is often a hardship to the nursing staff . . . The most marked results of the open-air life are shown during the first few months of stay in hospital . . . [children] soon become rosy-cheeked and contented, the appetite improves rapidly" (quoted in Morris and Priestley, *Journeys of Hope*, 135–36).

and described in 1919. In order to provide ventilation, children slept in dormitories which were deliberately kept draughty. Pamela's dormitory had brick walls no more than a yard high. The rest of the space up to the roof consisted of wire netting. The floor was concrete and the children slept on iron beds. The idea was to strengthen their lungs and stiffen their resistance to cold and hardship. In the winter, as snow and sleet blew through the wire mesh, the children would pull the beds into the center of the room and huddle away from the wind and ice. Pamela recalls how they were taken on walks along the seafront in order to benefit from the sea breeze and then put to bed for two hours during the day to recover.

Playtimes were restricted to half an hour a day, parental visits to an hour at most. Hugging or kissing was discouraged. To reach the hospital my parents caught a bus, two trains and another bus, only to sit at a table with Pam for an hour. When my father had to work on Saturdays our mother would visit accompanied by an aunt as she lacked the confidence to travel by train alone.

Children were not allowed to cry. If they cried or complained, they could be locked in a room with barred windows. Pamela remembers staring out through the bars, crying for our father to come and take her home. There were no beatings or threats of physical violence, but children were "sent to Coventry" for any misdemeanor.[11] This punishment involved complete isolation, effectively a form of solitary confinement. For a specified period, the child would be treated as though they did not exist. Any child who tried to contact them would suffer the same penalty themselves. Pamela recalls several occasions where she was shut away in a cupboard or small room, without food or drink, and not allowed to go to the bathroom. Once, she was so thirsty she drank her own urine.

One day Pamela escaped. She passed through the dormitory, into the corridor and out through the front door unobserved. The train station was only a few hundred yards away. She reasoned in her young mind that if only she could get on a train it would take her home. She boarded the first train to arrive and hid in the baggage compartment. By then, her absence was noticed. The nurses raised the alarm. Police delayed the train and searched each carriage. They found Pamela hiding among the luggage. Why had she run away? She did her best to explain. The hours locked in silent rooms, the

---

11. "Sent to Coventry" is a British colloquialism for being shunned or ostracized. It is said to derive from the civil wars of the 1640s when Royalist prisoners sent to the town by the Parliamentarians were shunned and ignored by the townspeople.

punishments, the restrictions, the abuse. No one listened. She was taken back to the hospital and found herself in a locked room once more. She lost all track of time. It was light when she entered the barred room, then dark and quiet, and light once more when they let her out.

There were twelve girls in Pam's dormitory. She was the only one to survive. Time after time the staff carried a small body to the morgue. Occasionally, some of the other girls managed to sneak in and hide underneath the bed where the body of a friend lay. So intense was their need for attachment and love. A close bond developed between the girls. While they were together, they were safe.

Pamela bonded particularly closely with a girl called Heather. They became best friends. One snowy night, as the girls drew the beds into the center of the dormitory, Pamela climbed into Heather's bed to keep her friend warm. When she woke up in the morning, Heather's body was as cold as ice. She had died during the night. Pamela was eight years old and her best friend died in bed beside her.

My parents knew none of this. Pamela wrote home using a standard form of words, a template provided by the hospital staff. She found a whole sheaf of these letters in a drawer after our mother died. Each one was almost the same as the others and almost exactly the same as those the other children wrote. Often the main text was written up on a chalkboard for the children to copy down. My sister says that anyone seeing her writing then, at the age of seven and eight, would assume it was written by a younger child. The inmates were only taught for two hours a day and at a very basic level, how to write their names, how to copy letters. Was it assumed that there was little point in educating them any further? They were not expected to survive.

My sister does have fond memories of some of the staff, particularly the matron who treated her kindly when news came that our Great Aunt Marie and then our Granny Pease had died. I was born at our Great Aunt Marie's house. Our parents could not afford to rent somewhere of their own at that time. So my grandfather's sister and her family took them in. Pamela remembers her hearty kindly laugh. It remains with her to this day and was one of the memories she clung to at the hospital—a warm, resonant laugh, the sound of family, the sound of home.

My mother's recollections of the matron were rather different. After four years without Pamela, my parents decided that enough was enough.

She had to come home. The matron traveled to Yorkshire by train to persuade my mother that Pamela should remain in hospital.

"You do know that if she comes home it will be the death of her," the matron said. "It'll all be your fault."

"Then if she dies, at least she'll die at home," my mother retorted.

Whether it was at our mother's insistence or, as Pamela believes, because the hospital needed the space, my sister came home. If the pain of separation had been intense, that of reunion was almost equally strong. Pamela was a very sick child. Worse, she came home cowed and institutionalized.

It was many years before any of us heard the full story of what had happened, but we felt the effects of it. Pamela was distant, reticent, subdued. She felt unable to ask for anything, shocked whenever she heard me asking for treats. She would rather steal than ask. She would sneak into the pantry and take cookies or candy. This was just one of the effects of life at the hospital. No one dared asked for anything.

Pamela would chuckle to herself when my mother warned me not to ask for things whenever we went to anyone's house. We had to wait until it was offered. We should never ask.

"But how will they know what I want if I don't ask?"

Pamela smiled at my childish logic but was inwardly terrified at the prospect of ever asking for anything or telling anyone how she felt.

Talking to Pamela years later I recognize all too well the classic symptoms of institutionalization. It is something I have seen time and time again around the world. I see children who have lost the ability to laugh or cry, who keep silent for fear of the consequences. I see children who have lost all spark and vivacity, children who turn in on themselves and find it hard to engage with others, children who are no longer children. They spend their time people watching just as Pamela tells me she did. They quietly observe what's going on to assess how best to survive.

For some years afterward, Pamela was convinced that if she did anything wrong the authorities would come and take her away. A doctor summoned her into his office the day she was discharged from hospital. Her parents were coming to fetch her, he told her. They were taking her home.

"But let me tell you this, Pamela Pease, if you tell anyone what has happened here, we know where to find you. We can come and take you back at any time."

She was also convinced that I "wanted her gone," that I resented her and wanted her to go back.

Pamela had good reason to think so. I did resent her. This sister I had only known from a photograph and from parental absences was now back and taking center stage. I was only around five or six years old when she came home and was used to being the focus of attention. She was a sickly child and I thought my parents handled her with kid gloves. She was always ill and lost a lot of time at school. I feigned illness to get attention or threw myself down the stairs in an attempt to avoid lessons. Whenever my sister became upset she would pant in short, choking gasps, a kind of asthmatic attack.

"Look what you've done! You've upset her now. You've brought on one of her turns!"

"She's putting it on. Can't you see? She's just shamming to get me into trouble!"

We were constantly fighting, constantly rowing. I was jealous of Pamela and she was jealous of me. I could play out longer in the summer—heat and hay fever meant that she stayed indoors for most of the summer months. I would also argue with my mother and answer her back. This would lead to blazing rows that subsided as quickly as they had started. Then we carried on as if nothing had happened. This also shocked Pamela. Years of enforced absence had taken its toll. She had only known the briefest contact with my parents, mostly one or other of them, rarely both together. Always in public, under scrutiny, across a table in a cold institution and behind closed doors.

I would come across almost identical situations as a social worker. Introducing a child to a foster family requires careful management. So does the process of reuniting a child with its biological family after a period of absence. What I experienced as a child when Pamela came home is exactly how many siblings react when an absent brother or sister returns. Family life changes during that period; sometimes other children are born or one parent leaves or dies and another appears. It's as if the child reenters their family stuck in time, the moment they left, and expects it to be the same. We had no help from social services or anyone else. We struggled through and learned to adjust. When I was nine we moved to Grandad Pease's house after he was killed riding his motorcycle home from church. The backdraft from a passing truck caused him to lose his balance. He struck his head on the drainpipe of one of the closely packed row houses. Grandad's house was larger than ours, we had more space, but times were still tough.

Pamela's childhood and teenage years were traumatic. Illness, separation and then, aged fourteen, she was beaten up by one of the gangs that roamed our estate. She crawled home in agony and subsequently had to have a kidney removed. She nearly died. A lad from our church visited her, left a note. They became friends. He helped her learn to read and write properly, eventually married her and supported her through her long years of recovery. The years of separation left their mark.

People ask whether my sister's experiences influenced what was to become my life's work. Was I on some kind of moral crusade? It did not feel like that at the time. Besides, I was later to work in institutional childcare without for a moment doubting its suitability or effectiveness. It is only in hindsight that I fully appreciate what it must have meant for Pamela. Perhaps that's why I feel so passionate about these issues, what it means for many children with similar experiences of loss, abuse, and neglect. Maybe that's why I sometimes get emotional when delivering training for potential foster parents, social and aid workers. This is not a job to me, it's a way of life, one that makes more and more sense the older I get. I increasingly appreciate just what it means for children who are so cruelly ignored, used, and abused.

Mam and Dad did their best for Pamela when she returned. My father made her a wooden doll's cot, the first gift she could ever remember that was entirely her own. He made it so well that the couple next door later used it for their baby. Pamela treasured it, the first thing that was ever hers and not for sharing with the entire dormitory. At last, she was safe. She was home.

3. Life Lessons

YOU WERE JUST ANOTHER AUTHORITY FIGURE
TELLING HIM WHAT TO DO.

WHEN EDDIE ROUNDED ON me I felt as if I were staring into the eyes of a cornered beast. His reaction took me completely by surprise with its sudden ferocity and venom.

"Who do you think you are? Do you think you are bigger than us, cleverer than us?" I could feel his breath on my face as he jabbed and prodded at my chest.

"Eddie . . . Eddie . . ."

"You want to watch out, that's all. You want to watch your back, I could have you, I could break your arms!"

"Eddie, there's no need to . . ."

"And those kids of yours, you watch out for those lads because if I catch them, I'll break their arms and all!"

That was it. Nobody threatened my boys. A red light flashed in front of my eyes.

"Why you . . . !"

Eddie broke away, stormed out of the TV lounge and down the stairs. I followed him, enraged. I wanted my pound of flesh.

To think of all the time I had invested in this lad. I had drawn close to him, connected in a way that none of the other staff had been able to. One of the supervisors at the care home had noticed it.

"Mick, whatever it is you are doing with Eddie, just keep doing it. I don't know what you've done, but you are the first member of staff he has ever opened up to."

"'I've just spent time with him, that's all,' I replied, rather pleased that my efforts had not gone unnoticed. "Drawn alongside him, kicked a football around, gone running."

"Well, however you've done it, you are the first person ever to get through to him," the supervisor said. "Keep it up. It's good work."

Now, here was Eddie scuttling down the stairs with me in pursuit. My blood was up. When he turned I let him have it, not physically, but verbally, all my anger, all my frustration. How I felt, how he had let me down. How disappointed I was, how hurt I felt. Me, me, me.

Eddie hauled his hurt and anger away into the night and as my pulse and breathing slowed, it suddenly hit me. What had I done? I was the first person Eddie had ever trusted and I had thrown it back in his face. I told him how angry I was, without any consideration of his feelings. I had belittled him in front of other people, made him feel worthless.

We were residential houseparents in a care home at Sutton Coldfield in the English Midlands. Princess Alice Orphanage was established in 1883 by National Children's Home (NCH),[1] an organization with Methodist roots. It was laid out on the "cottage homes" model, with houses grouped around a large green. It had an imposing clock tower, a chapel, and, originally, workshops to teach the children useful trades. At first, the children lived in single-sex "family groups" of up to thirty, each supervised by a "house-mother."[2] During the Second World War, the number of children swelled to over 300 as orphanages in the cities closed under the threat of German bombing. By the time we arrived in 1979, the numbers had dropped to around 120. Some additional children's houses had been added in the 1950s, but by that time, trends favored smaller groups. Typically, there would be ten to twelve children in a house and the accommodation was now mixed sex. We had up to eighteen teenagers in the adolescent unit.

We were impressed. There was plenty of space, the green acted as a play area, and the way the cottages were organized made sense. As you looked around the green you could follow the progression from babies in one house to toddlers and preschool children in the next, then five- to seven-year-olds, then seven- to ten-year-olds, and on it went with accommodation for adolescents. It was all very neat, all very sequential. At that time, we saw nothing wrong with it.

---

1. National Children's Home is now called Action for Children. It now looks for family-based alternatives to residential care. See https://www.actionforchildren.org.uk/.

2. Higginbotham, "Princess Alice," lines 15–16.

Already the tide was beginning to turn against large residential care homes. Local authorities were looking at adoption and foster care as alternatives. The older and larger orphanages were expensive to maintain. They had funding problems. There had always been informal alternatives to residential care. People often took over the care of children of deceased or absent relatives. Funding was temporarily available in the form of "parish relief" for abandoned mothers or single parents. Yet for generations, poorer people lived under the shadow of the workhouse.[3]

The practice of fostering developed during Victorian times, where a child might live temporarily with another family until a more permanent arrangement could be found. By the end of the nineteenth century, the UK's poor law authorities and voluntary agencies increasingly used fostering or "boarding out" as an alternative to orphanages or the dreaded workhouse system. The Victorians drew a distinction between the "deserving" and "undeserving" poor. The workhouses were not penal institutions but were often made as sparse and unpleasant as possible to deter "the indigent" or "the work-shy" from becoming a burden on the parish or the state. Generations of the working poor lived in fear of ending their lives in the workhouse. Conditions were equally grim for younger people in these institutions so it is hardly surprising that the first orphanages were greeted as welcome alternatives.

Adoption became increasingly common during and after the First World War and the first official legislation to regulate the process was passed in 1926. This process continues to the present day with successive legislation aiming to correct previous imbalances or to protect the rights of the child. There have been seismic changes in social and cultural attitudes, of course, particularly from the 1960s. Back then adopted children were largely the offspring of unmarried mothers who gave up their children rather than face the social stigma. As social attitudes shifted and as divorce and remarriage became more common, legal frameworks adapted to reflect the change. The number of adoptions in the UK peaked in 1968 and has declined steadily since, reflecting dramatic social change. A child adopted in the UK today is more likely to have been in local authority care because they are considered to be "at risk" of neglect or abuse.

---

3. The workhouse developed as a form of poor relief from the sixteenth and seventeenth centuries onward. After the 1834 Poor Law Amendment Act the system became a deterrent against would-be paupers and claimants. Conditions were made as grim and Spartan as possible. See Higginbotham, "Introduction," lines 30–50.

For a variety of reasons, the days of the old-fashioned orphanage were numbered. Society had changed and the institutions had failed to keep pace. We were blissfully unaware of the changes looming for institutions like Princess Alice Drive, as it was then known. We could see that money was tight. We could see that funding and sponsorship would decrease. We could not foresee that the home would close in the early 1980s. As far as we were concerned it was a steady job and one we were likely to enjoy. Brenda did much of the cooking and the caring, we got on well with the domestic staff, a truly great bunch of people. We kept records, arranged visits, and protected the children's welfare. We chased after them when they ran away. There was space for our two boys to run around and we had accommodation. We thought we had it made. We had a regular wage, a roof over our heads, and were perhaps, at last, fulfilling our mission to help others.

As it turned out, our time at Princess Alice Drive proved to be among the hardest of my life. It was the closest I ever came, according to both Brenda and John Ellerington, to a nervous breakdown. The confrontation with Eddie nearly pushed me over the edge.

We entered residential childcare by a roundabout route—Bible college.

"Leaving t'pit? What are you doing that for? Where're you going?" asked the men at the coalface at Kellingley Colliery.

"Bible college. The Birmingham Bible Institute."

"*Bible college?* Hey up Mick the Vic', we knew you were religious, but we didn't know you wanted to be a proper vicar!"

Mick the Vic' was my nickname at the coalface and in the pit-head baths on account of my faith.

"I don't want to become a vicar."

"What then? A missionary?"

"I'm not sure I want to do that either."

"Then what are you going to Bible college *for*?"

If I was honest, I had no idea.

All I did know was that I had a sense that I wanted to make a difference, to do something with my life that involved more than working, earning money, and going on vacation. It started at one of the Bible conventions we attended at Filey on the Yorkshire coast. I first met Brenda there and we continued to attend during our courtship and early years of marriage. Each year, from 1955, some 8,000 people or so would gather at Butlins vacation

experiment. Rather than sitting the examination, pupils would be assessed by the accumulated average of their grades across the year. Somehow, I had scraped through! I was off to Castleford Grammar. I had arrived and I had a bike to prove it.

In the event, I struggled at grammar school. I had no interest in Latin or the other subjects on the traditional curriculum. It's a shame I didn't pay more attention to languages though, given my later travels. After a French test where I scored seven or eight marks out of a hundred, the teacher took me aside.

"I gave you five of those because you'd turned up and put your name on the paper."

I was good at spelling and English, brilliant at sport, but that was about it. One year my science teacher wrote in my school report, "He is lazy."

"Well, that's it then," my mother said on reading it. "It can't get any worse than that!"

The following year, with the same tutor, the report read, "He is bone idle."

I had done it! I had exceeded even the damning report of the previous year. I had graduated from being "lazy" to "bone idle" and was very proud of myself.

Eventually, the school conceded defeat. It was possible to leave at fifteen in those days and they told me that I was wasting my own time as well as everyone else's. I would be better applying to technical college. There I could learn a trade and prepare for work in the foundries or mines. So I applied to Whitwood Technical College, only to be refused entry. My cousin Catherine worked in the office there and saw the reference the school supplied. She told my mother in embarrassment that it was the worst she had ever known them receive.

We contested the decision. The College relented and let me in. For the first time, I began to do well and before long I was an apprentice mechanic at Kellingley Colliery.

I enjoyed working down the mine. I liked the banter, the strong bond and camaraderie between men who worked in hard, physical conditions. I enjoyed the challenge of making equipment work in the dank, dark conditions far underground. Kellingley was known for the width of its coal seams, at around six feet among the widest in Britain. Neighboring pits had seams just eighteen inches to two feet wide. To work them, miners lay on their sides to pick at the coalface. Kellingley was fully mechanized, but conditions were still challenging. The floors of the seams were so soft that the metal props sank into them. We often worked in cramped spaces. The place was tough and the talk was ripe. I was no prude, but for a young man with evangelical convictions, the language and stories could get a bit much. Men teased others during late shifts that colleagues from earlier shifts were even now around at their houses visiting their wives. If you were different in any way you became a target. You might be deemed too fat or too thin, too short or too tall, or you had spots, ginger hair, very curly or straight hair, wore glasses—whatever it was, your colleagues homed in on it. It was incessant. It could be harmless and funny at times. Often it was merciless. You had to be resilient and confident in yourself. You had to stand your ground. Many couldn't face the relentless baiting and found other work.

This was the work and world I knew, so to leave all that and apply to Bible college was to enter a completely new dimension. Undeterred by Elim's rejection, I persisted. The more applications I made, the more rejections I received. I began to lose hope. Perhaps I had got it wrong. Then, one day, success—an acceptance letter arrived. We were going to the Birmingham Bible Institute.[5] Perhaps our calling was reaching fulfillment.

Birmingham Bible Institute valued fire and fervency. We certainly had plenty of that. I'd burned Mrs. Gardner's curtains and worked in the intense heat of the coalface. The Institute was founded by a colorful Presbyterian minister called Henry Brash Bonsall. He preached an old-fashioned hot gospel. One tutor paraded around in a sandwich board calling upon people to repent. Brenda was required to enroll alongside me and took her two-year course over three years due to family commitments. For all the fervor there was certainly some academic rigor. We had to learn some New Testament Greek and church history, the kinds of subjects I had balked at during my school days. Most importantly for what was to come, it taught me how to study. Nobody had shown me how to approach a textbook, how to make notes in lectures, how to research and present my arguments, so I asked Pamela's husband, Brian, to help me prepare for study.

We loved the community life at the college, the close fellowship with other families. We made long-lasting friendships. The discipline of study stood us in good stead too for what we were to do later, but even as stalwart Pentecostals, we found the fieriness and fervency hard to take. Not only

---

5. Now Birmingham Christian College, see http://bccoll.uk/about-us/.

was it presented in a style more fitting for the 1930s or '50s, but everything seemed bound by petty rules and regulations.

"Why didn't we see you at the early morning prayer meeting, brother?"

"Because I've got young boys and they were up sick in the night."

"The meetings must come first, brother."

"What, with young children running a temperature? You have to be kidding!"

We lived at the top of a tall Victorian tenement block, sharing a confined space close to another family studying at the Institute. Our room was a combined kitchen, dining room, lounge, and bedroom. It was so cold in winter that the glass door on our wall cabinet iced over.

Our two boys slept in a small separate bedroom and had to run all the way downstairs to play outside. Sometimes the other family would leave their belongings on the landing and our lads would play with them or throw them down the stairs. Like me, Mark and Kevin loved the outdoors and loved playing sport, but whenever I kicked a ball around with them on the grass or we tried to play cricket, someone told us to stop.

"No ball games. You know the rules."

"I've got two young lads here. What am I supposed to play with them?"

"Frisbee."

"Frisbee? How come it's alright to throw a frisbee around on the grass but not kick a ball about?"

"Those are the rules."

So, here I was again, up against petty rules and regulations. We were adults and yet we felt treated like kids. When our third and final year came we were still no wiser as to what we were going to do at the end of the course. We became close friends with Richard and Paula, a couple at the Institute, who suggested we apply for a position as residential care helpers at Princess Alice Drive.

Paula said to me suddenly, out of the blue, "You'd make a good social worker."

"What do social workers do?" I asked. By this time, I was twenty-eight years old.

Richard and Paula's background lay in probation and social work and they felt we were ideally cut out for work of this kind. Again, it was an example of someone coming along at the right time and providing a prompting and direction when we most needed it. Without it, we may not have gone into the children's home and from there onto my social work training and the work we do now.

We learned a lot at Birmingham Bible Institute. We learned how to live in close proximity to other people and how to study. I passed my O level English at the Institute, the first academic qualification I ever gained.[6] We were also exposed to other cultures and made friends from around the world, some of whom we still see. During a road trip to Greece immediately after the course, we saw poverty at a much deeper level than we had seen in the UK. Passing through the former Yugoslavia we saw people living in crumbling houses and primitive conditions, working their meager farms by hand. It was still the Communist era and we experienced the bleakness and drabness I would not see again until my trips to Romania after the fall of Ceauşescu.

After the rigidity of the Bible Institute, the broad lawns and cottage-style accommodation at Princess Alice Drive seemed heaven sent. The home was in the leafy suburbs of Birmingham, near Solihull, where the James Bond actor Roger Moore once had a house. There was plenty of space, a great atmosphere, and wonderful people to work with. We were on our feet at last.

We had much more to learn. Residential social care proved to be our toughest test yet. The children came from poor and disadvantaged backgrounds. Many had suffered abuse and neglect. The teenagers were the hardest of all—unruly, rebellious, and prone to breakouts, vandalism, and sometimes violence. Eddie was one of the hardest to reach. He was slightly built and unkempt, rarely spoke and hardly ever made eye contact. He seemed to slouch and shuffle around, dragging his own pain. We shared a common interest in soccer. He was a big fan of West Bromwich Albion, nicknamed "The Baggies," one of the leading Midlands teams. Whenever I mentioned them his eyes lit up, he lifted his gaze and become animated. We discussed individual players, league results, goals. He was a lad transformed. I often jogged around the grounds and nearby streets. One day Eddie asked to come with me. I agreed. We went out jogging together regularly after that, not talking about anything in particular, simply enjoying the fresh air and exercise. People noticed a difference. Eddie was coming out of his shell.

One day I returned to Princess Alice Drive from visiting a teenager in hospital to find Brenda concerned and agitated. There had been an incident

6. The General Certificate of Education (GCE) Ordinary Level was the standard qualification before leaving secondary school in the UK for many years and generally considered equivalent to the US High School Diploma.

in the TV room. The teenagers were playing loud music. They refused to turn it down, became boisterous and aggressive. Things got out of hand. They had set fire to the litter bins and trashed the room. I was told Eddie was the ringleader.

"Eddie?" I was annoyed and aghast. I hadn't expected this kind of behavior from him. Not now I had got through to him, befriended him, won him around.

I set off to give him a piece of my mind.

In front of a number of his friends, I said, "Eddie, what's all this about? You should know better."

It was then he turned on me. It was then that I made my biggest mistake.

"You realize what just happened, don't you?" the supervisor said as we met in his office some days later. "Eddie trusted and opened up to you. He shared the angry feelings he had about life and his family and you threw it back in his face. You belittled him in front of the others. That's why he erupted. He thought you understood him, that he could trust you as a friend. Now you were just another authority figure telling him what to do."

I put my head in my hands. The supervisor was right. It wasn't that Eddie should be allowed to get away with setting fire to the bins and stirring up the other kids. My mistake was in the way I had challenged him, how I had abused his trust. If there was one thing I was to learn from my time in residential care, my subsequent social work studies, and work in child protection, it is the importance of significant relationships. Strong, significant relationships provide an anchor for children in biological families. They provide an anchor for children in substitute families too or any other context we might think of. It applies the world over. Strong relationships give us the security we need. Without people we can trust to protect, guide, and provide for us, the world becomes a scary place. Even as adults we need to feel safe. Relationships provide this sense of security. Through relationships, we learn to handle the adversities, difficulties, and complexities of life. As children, we do that with parents or primary care providers. If they do not provide this support consistently, we struggle to cope and provide for ourselves. What starts as an innate need for food, warmth, and protection as a child continues into adulthood. We require affection, security, guidance, the provision of physical needs. I have never forgotten that incident with Eddie. I tell it in training and briefing sessions to this day. It was one of the biggest life lessons I ever learned.

4. Following the Call

DON'T LET IT DIE!

"So João, what would you recommend I do if I want to work with street kids and in child protection here in Brazil?"

João Bosco de Carvalho, an experienced Brazilian children's worker, raised his eyebrows. A sardonic smile spread across his face.

"Learn Portuguese?"[1]

We both laughed but recognized the serious point. It wasn't what we wanted to hear but knew instinctively that it was right. We had both seen too many well-meaning aid workers or missionaries bumbling along with no grasp of the language and culture.

We learned Portuguese. Rachel Thornton, a languages student at Leeds University, gave Brenda and I some coaching before we set off for Brazil in 1997. Rachel met her husband Richard while they were both missionaries in Brazil. Richard later worked as an accountant and they returned to Brazil for a few years through a job exchange. They joke that I was to stay in their spare room so often during my regular visits to Brazil that they named it "The Suite Pease."[2]

We also enrolled on an evening class. For over a year we grappled with the grammar and pronunciation. Our good friend and collaborator, family lawyer Ranjit Uppal, laughs as he tells of how truly impressive our grasp of the language came to be. One afternoon under a blazing Brazilian sun, as Ranjit and his wife Raj accompanied me on a training and advocacy visit, I confidently ordered a light meal at a restaurant. One by one the plates kept

---

1. João married an English missionary. The story of their work with Brazilian street children is recorded in De Carvalho, *Street Children of Brazil*.

2. Richard and Rachel Maingot, in discussion with Philip Williams, April 29, 2018.

coming. Soon the table was groaning under the weight of main courses and side dishes. Instead of ordering the lightest option, I had ordered a banquet!

If I was to struggle with language on my later visits to Brazil, I was struggling with accents during our last months in the English Midlands. I have often joked that I knew our time there was at an end when I heard Mark and Kevin picking up the regional accent, the slow, almost lethargic "Brummie" drawl.[3] It was then I knew we had to move back to Yorkshire. I wanted my lads to have the "broad Yorkshire" accent and to support Leeds United![4]

It was more than homesickness and regional pride that drew us back north. My time working at the residential home was the toughest of my career. The incident with Eddie had affected me deeply. The kids were lovely in so many ways, but for me, unruly, cheeky, and hard to deal with. We were on call 24/7. I was nearing burnout.

Once a week I rang John Ellerington at a public call box at a prearranged time. He did not have a telephone at home. In the cold and wet he walked faithfully to the call box to listen to me unload. He remembers hearing the dejection in my voice. What were we doing in Birmingham? We knew few people. We had no family there, few friends.

"I've a mind to jack it all in, John," I told him. "Come back up north. Go back down the pit."

I did once ask the pit managers if they would have me back. We even put our names on a public housing list and the boys on a school list expecting to return to Yorkshire. Once again, things worked out differently to how we had planned.

"Living in" at the children's home was very stressful. I could cope with the early afternoons. Those were my times for writing up notes and reports, but as the evenings approached and the children returned from school, my stress levels rose. I knew there would be an issue or an incident. Kids often ran away while I was on night duty and I'd call the police out to look for them.

---

3. The distinctive West Midlands accent centered on Birmingham and its "Black Country" variant around nearby Dudley and Wolverhampton, ranks among Britain's least favorite regional accents in nationwide polls. A YouGov poll of over 2,000 Britons in 2014 placed the Brummie accent at the bottom of the list (Dahlgreen, "'Brummie'"). There are good-natured regional rivalries around speech and accents in the UK, which has a surprising variety for a relatively small country.

4. "Broad Yorkshire" is the term used for the strongest Yorkshire accents. Leeds United was then one of the UK's leading soccer teams and carrying all before it.

"Lock them up," the local police would say, exasperated at yet another call.

"Lock them up? Why? They're not criminals."

"Then you get out after them, stop calling us out all the time!"

I recall another time chatting in a nearby bar with some players from a squash league I joined. One asked me where I worked so I pointed across the road toward Princess Alice Drive.

"What? With those unruly kids? What have they done to end up inside there?"

I retorted that most of them had done nothing wrong. They were the innocent victims of inappropriate adult behavior. "They aren't the problem, their families are!"

No matter how much the kids stretched me, I always defended them.

Brenda had less hassle with them. She was like a mother figure. They would push back at me, try to move the boundaries, test me out to see how far they could go. It was all to do with rejection, of course. They opposed authority figures in order to assert their own sense of individuality or self-worth. So around 3:30 p.m., come rain or shine I went for a walk to clear my head and prepare for whatever the evening held.

There were people I could turn to for help. Brenda remembers my talking things through with the minister of Sutton Baptist Church. There was William, a Ghanaian friend from Bible college. There was John in Yorkshire, listening to me in a call box until I ran out of change.

I realized that we needed to move out. We had lived on-site alongside the children for two years. The stress was becoming too much. We wanted to continue working at the home but wanted to find somewhere to live nearby—but where? This was one of the most expensive areas in the Midlands. House prices were beyond our reach and renting options were few unless we were prepared to move further away.

We received a local authority grant to go to Bible college, something very unusual at that time. After the three-year Bible college course and our road trip to Greece, we were penniless. We had around £4 left, a little over $5 at today's exchange rates. The job at Princess Alice Drive came with free accommodation, Brenda was paid, and there were no utility bills. We could also eat with the kids so expenses were low. We bought a car and a trailer, which we kept at a trailer park near Kidderminster to stay on those weekends when we were not on duty. It gave us much-needed respite a short distance from the children's home. It saved us having to drive all the way to

Brenda's family in Devon or mine in Yorkshire on those precious weekends when we were not working.

I was desperately looking for options for my family. One day the superintendent of the children's home called me over. He had been speaking to the home's chaplain, the minister of Streetly Methodist Church. They had a vacancy as the janitor was suddenly leaving after twenty years' service. The position came with free accommodation on-site. Were we interested?

Streetly Methodist Church was very active in the community. Scouts and other groups used its community hall during the week. It was hired for weddings and other events. The job was ideal for Brenda with her organizational skills. She dealt with the hall bookings for weddings and funerals, prepared the venue, ensured everything ran smoothly, and cleaned and tidied afterward. I could cycle into work. The church was no more than two or three miles from the children's home so I could maintain my job without the stress of living on-site. It was a godsend.

The number of children referred to Princess Alice Drive was decreasing. Residential care homes depended on local government for their intake of children. The more children they looked after the more income they received. If a local authority could not afford to build or maintain its own residential accommodation, it would place the children with independent care providers. The system was volatile and precarious. If a local authority cut its budget, the independent providers suffered. So did the children. They were passed from pillar to post, from bed to bed, from hostel to home. All too often it was a question of budgets, economies, and cuts. The children would be removed to whichever option presented the lowest cost.

There was, and remains, a continuous ebb and flow of referrals of children from local authority care out into the private or independent sector. These days the independent providers are largely fostering agencies rather than residential homes. The few remaining residential homes generally accommodate children with specific physical, emotional, or behavioral needs, or those who have lost faith in any form of family life following repeated rejection. Children are still moved around both local authority and private systems in a way that creates insecurity and stress.

By now, even though we could see a decline in the number of children entering residential care, I was convinced that some form of social care with children was the way I should go. What were the implications, though, if the days of large-scale residential homes were numbered?

I wanted to remain in social care but was unsure how to proceed. I made inquiries to the probation service and other agencies. They told me I needed qualifications. I knew there was a social work course at what was then Birmingham Polytechnic and applied for it. I discovered that each year the NCH provided paid seconded placements for members of staff aiming for further or professional qualifications. These placements were generally reserved for staff in middle management or senior positions. I was in neither. It was a long shot, but I went for it. I was so convinced that I would somehow gain a place that I told everyone I was starting in September. I would even point to the large concrete building as we drove in and out of Birmingham and "tell it" that I was on my way! Our sons thought it was hilarious, me talking to a concrete building!

The application process involved interviews, tests, and group exercises. I could see that I was up against people with far more experience. I met people who had worked their way up to superintendent or management level and who now needed a professional qualification in their field. The tutors were very encouraging. They told me that they always welcomed mature students as this gave the course balance and provided role models for the younger applicants. It did them good to hear from people who had experience in the field. I told them of my experience at the children's home, about the incident with Eddie.

"Exactly," they said. "This is precisely the sort of experience that the younger students lack, for all their academic qualifications and drive."

I was accepted onto the course, but there was only one snag—money.

How was I going to pay for it? Tuition fees had yet to be introduced for publicly funded higher education in the UK, but we still needed to live.

We had few savings. We sold our mobile home, and lost money on it, over £1,000, a large sum in those days.

"Never mind," the admissions tutors said. "You can apply again for next year. We can hold a place open for you while you raise the funds."

At Princess Alice Drive I was told that the policy had changed. NCH was no longer providing paid placements, but there were grants available, just six for the entire country. It was an even longer shot now. I applied. I was turned down.

"Never mind, Mick," my supervisor said. "They have put you on the reserve list."

"A miss is as good as a mile," I thought, but even then, maintained the hope I'd get to Poly in September.

One day, as I pulled up on my bike, ready to start work, the deputy superintendent, appeared and called me over to his office.

He was all smiles.

"Mick, your name has come up. You've got the grant! Someone must have dropped out and they've decided to give it to you!"

I was stunned. "What? That's fantastic, how did that happen?"

"I have no idea," he said. "But I can tell you that your name was nowhere near the top of the reserve list."

"I knew it!" I cried. "I knew I would get on the course somehow."

I felt my prayers were answered, my expectations fulfilled.

I was delighted. At long last, I was training and studying for something that might help me make a difference and do something significant and worthwhile. Bible college had paved the way, taught me how to study. The practical experience at Princess Alice Drive augmented that. Then, after two years of grueling social work study, research, practice placements, and the presentation of numerous papers, I had a professional qualification. I was motoring.

We returned to Yorkshire when I qualified. NCH had a residential facility at Bramhope near Leeds. I was part of a small social work team that worked both within the children's home and out across Leeds and up into North Yorkshire. A condition of the grant was that I remained with the organization for two years after gaining my social work qualification. In the event, as their Yorkshire operation downscaled, I moved over to the social work department of Leeds City Council.

Leeds is the largest city in the West Yorkshire conurbation. It dominates the region. With its universities, teaching hospitals, vibrant financial, legal and service sectors, it was and remains a major hub for business, culture, and sport. Even though I had grown up barely sixteen miles away, I did not know it very well. I knew Elland Road, the home of Leeds United. I knew the main shopping mall. That was all. The parts I liked were the northern fringes, small towns like Otley and Ilkley. I loved their distinctive stone houses and views over the Yorkshire Dales. We soon found that the house prices were beyond our reach. We had to look further into the city, then further in again. Eventually, we found a place we felt was right, a small semidetached house in Armley, just two miles out of Leeds city center. It had a small, old-fashioned kitchen. The whole house needed attention, but we somehow knew it was home. We soon settled in and joined a large and lively church which was doing good work on our side of the city at that time. We made connections there that have stayed with us; Andrew and Alison Grimshaw, Pete and Sheila White, John and Joy Swift. I was to go on relief trips to Romania with some of these guys. Once again, I found people I connected with who became important and significant friends.

It was 1989. The Iron Curtain came down. One by one the states of the former Soviet bloc were breaking loose. Dick Syms, once pastor of the church we attended in Leeds, had moved to York. Dick became involved with relief trips to Romania after the fall of Ceauşescu but before the conditions in Romanian orphanages caused global outrage. He remembers being shown around one by the nurses. Conditions were basic, but the nurses put on as good a show as they could. When he got back to the truck he found he had left his jacket behind by mistake. When he went to retrieve it, he found something very different. The nurses were not expecting him. It was bedlam. He saw babies and children lying unattended in cots, wallowing in their own filth. They were screaming, crying, fighting. No one was taking any notice.[5] Scenes like this were later broadcast around the world. There was an international outcry and a rush to provide aid.

Andrew Grimshaw was galvanized. He wanted to help. We could take truckloads over with aid and supplies. I was skeptical at first. Where was the money? We didn't know how to go about it, where would we start? We invited Dick over to talk to us and share his experience. After much preparation and fundraising, we booked two weeks' vacation and set off, Andrew Grimshaw, Pete White, and myself, with a truckload of supplies.

We had secondhand clothes, doctors' uniforms, nurses' uniforms, bric-a-brac and children's toys. We took bandages and medical supplies. We took walking frames, crutches, wheelchairs, and these were very gratefully received. We were particularly proud of the electronic typewriter someone donated, convinced it would impress the Romanians and make a difference. We later found that the voltage was incompatible and that there were no spare parts. The typewriter was completely useless.

It was a three day drive, across to France, through Germany, down through central Europe. We drove fifteen hours a day, stopped for a beer and a bite to eat then headed off the next morning. There was initial confusion as we reached Cluj-Napoca and were unable to get in touch with Dick's main contact, Zolly (Zoltan), someone he had met quite by chance on the

5. Dick Syms, in discussion with Philip Williams, March 23, 2018.

border during his first trip. We spent the night in the truck. I drew the short straw and slept in the back with the supplies.

When we did contact Zolly and his family, we were as overwhelmed by the welcome they gave us as Dick was previously. We were also astonished at the level of poverty and deprivation. We had asked Dick how much money to take. We wanted to buy souvenirs. He shook his head.

"Don't take anything," he warned. "There's nothing to spend it on. Take ten pounds if you must, fifteen at the most, but I suspect you'll bring most of it back with you."

Dick was right. The shelves were empty. There were some ceramics and mass-produced "crafts," local wine, old Soviet photographic equipment, but that was all. If we were surprised at the lack of shopping opportunities for tourist souvenirs, that was nothing compared to our shock at the living conditions the Romanians endured. After years of Communist rule, the country was drab, gray, and depressed. There was a lack of color and vitality, and worse, a lack of even the basic necessities.

Before we awoke, Zolly's brother got up at 5 a.m. to join the line for bread. People lined up for three hours for a loaf. When they brought it to us, Pete shook his head and put it aside, "I can't eat it."

"Why not? Because it's too hard and dry?"

The bread was unappetizing, to say the least. It had the texture of concrete. We may as well have been nibbling at the walls of Birmingham Polytechnic!

"No, because they've been queuing from five o'clock this morning for a single loaf of bread and now they are giving it to us. It's all they have!"

Each evening our Romanian hosts would share their meager rations with us and then disappear into the kitchen to eat what was left. We pleaded with them to stop. We had not come to eat them out of house and home. Yet they insisted. We were guests. We would insult them if we did not accept what hospitality they had.

I met Zolly again in 2016. He was in the UK for a conference. I was still embarrassed about some of the stuff we brought over in those days, the typewriter which did not work, the useless equipment, kindly meant but inappropriate.

He held up his hand. "Never, ever think that; what was rubbish to you was salvation to us."

It was another valuable lesson. These days we ensure that our charity identifies genuine need, rather than try to second-guess it. If we want to help, it is vital we provide the right kind of help. That we meet real rather than imagined needs. We cannot presume to know what those are unless we ask. That is a critical principle in the work I do now.

We made four trips to Romania and saw things gradually change. Mercedes and BMWs began to appear on the roads. Prosperity returned and with it the darker side, drugs, pornography. It was a lesson in how development brings both positive and negative effects and creates further problems, further needs. The first time we visited Romania there was no entertainment other than state TV. Yet Zolly and his family played all kinds of musical instruments—the guitar, bass, keyboard, cornet—in the National Youth Orchestra. They could each speak around four or five languages.

I once asked him, "How can you do all this? How did you become so accomplished in these fields?"

"What else were we to do?" he asked. "We had nothing we could do, nowhere to go. What we could do was learn."

I was deeply affected. These people had so few opportunities and yet they had achieved so much. I'd been presented with opportunities for education, opportunities galore. Yet, time and again, I turned them down. Only gradually did I come to appreciate its value and to apply myself. There were times when to use an extra light bulb in Romania laid families open to harassment or even criminal charges. Yet despite the deprivation and the political repression, this family achieved so much. To me it illustrates the strength of the family unit, the richness of relationships, the potential people have even in the harshest conditions.

I have often thought about this. We have only one life, one shot at things. Zolly and his family had nothing, only a few clothes, their musical instruments, and a tiny apartment. Yet they made the most of what they had. What is more, they shared it with others. They shared it with us.

Romania was my first experience of international aid work. It was not social work, but it set me thinking about the way I could apply my professional experience to the situations I had seen. People are surprised to hear that I only saw one of the huge Romanian orphanages that drew so much international attention. It was in Constanţa and it was appalling. Like most people at that time, I gleaned much of my information from the TV coverage. I did visit hospitals, hospices, and some children's homes. Children were living in dreary, soulless orphanages. They needed families.

The team I was part of at Leeds City Council specialized in childcare and was responsible for issues around adoption and fostering. We carried out background checks and assessed and trained foster parents. We ran training and awareness sessions for other social workers, informing them of the legal, procedural, and child development issues. We worked well as a team. My long-suffering supervisor, Valerie Hales, who became a close colleague and friend, remembers trying to rein me in at times when my quips in case meetings went too far.[6] I had a tendency to prod at anything I took to be pompous, bureaucratic, or stuffy. When it came to fighting someone's corner this could be appropriate, although I am sure my colleagues did not always appreciate it at times. The Yorkshire humor can be very dry and often blunt. I had to learn tact and diplomacy.

We were a small, committed team and I would like to think we made a difference. The training aspect was new to me. I had never delivered any training before. I hadn't read any books about it nor attended a course on how to train effectively. Yet here I was expected to train potential foster carers. "I hate it!" I said to Brenda. "It eats into the time we have for casework."

I complained to my bosses. Leeds City Council had professional training staff. Surely, they should be the ones to deliver training?

Their answer put me in my place. "Mick, you are a qualified social worker. You understand fostering and adoption. You know the processes and procedures. You can't expect general trainers to understand all that. It's a complex and specialist area. Who better to provide the training than the specialists themselves?"

In 1996 my father passed away after a three-month struggle with cancer. He told my sister Pamela that he knew "this was it." He had survived many serious accidents and illnesses, but he knew his time had come. When we were children he fell almost thirty feet through some faulty scaffolding, hitting his head on the planks on the way down. Boom! Boom! Boom! He fractured his skull and was not expected to survive. He pulled through but was off work for a year. The fault resulted from negligence and he eventually received compensation. It was the first and only time a small financial windfall ever fell into the Pease household! Dad lost his sense of taste and smell and Pamela remembers a distinct change in his personality too. Always a man of few words he spoke even less, he became somber and withdrawn. Later, in a serious collision, he was thrown through a car

---

6. Valerie Hales, in discussion with Philip Williams, January 29, 2018.

windscreen, losing flesh from his earlobes and suffering severe bleeding and serious scars. Again, he survived.

Pamela visited Dad on the cancer ward and read to him from the Bible. One day, after she'd gone, a patient leaned over toward my father from his bed.

"How can she believe in God after what happened to us?" he asked.

"Why? What happened?"

"I was in that hospital at the same time as Pamela," the man revealed. "In one of the boys' wards."

From this patient my father heard what had happened for the first time. "It ruined my life. It spoiled my marriage. It wrecked everything and there's your daughter spouting to you all about God!"

The next day my father asked Pamela about it.

"Pam, what that man told me, did it happen to you?"

Pamela took a deep breath. "Yes, Dad, it did."

She was wheeling my father out in his wheelchair for some fresh air. He had been sent home from hospital shortly before his death.

He gripped her hand. "Don't say anything to your Mam. Leave that with me."

By this time Pamela had begun to share her story at churches and fellowship groups. A tape recording of her account was in circulation. People known to my parents heard it. Eventually, our mother heard it too. Pamela believes that Dad had prepared her for it so that it came as less of a shock. Ever faithful, ever practical, he observed, "It's like the story of Joseph, our Pam. 'What was intended for harm, God intended for good.'[7] You're now able to help other people because of what happened, people who've been through the same sort of thing. Get your testimony out there, it can help others."

Dad did not live to see our year in Brazil and all that developed from that, but he knew of my first fact-finding and consultancy visits. To the end, he was keen that we fulfilled the call we'd felt so many years before.

"Mick," he said to me on his deathbed. "Your sense of mission, don't let it die, will you? Don't let it die."

We had various pastors and leaders in our church in Leeds, among them an American couple, Don and June Silber. They encouraged and supported us as we developed a soup run for homeless people. They always showed an interest in my trips to Romania, my concern for abandoned

7. Paraphrase of Gen 50:20 NIV.

and vulnerable children. It was through their son, David, a drummer with a Christian band, that we first heard about the mission station near São Paulo. When Don and June returned to the US in 1996 they had quite a send-off. The line of people waiting to thank and wish them well stretched out of the main auditorium and into the foyer. As we embraced them that last time, Don said to me, "Mick, your sense of mission, that call you have. Don't forget it, will you? Don't let it die."

5. Turning Point

IF I COULD CHANGE ONE THING, IT WOULD BE THIS.
I WANT A MOTHER OR A FATHER.

—MICK'S STORY, SFAC[1]

"NOW LET ME ASK you one more question," I said to the older children through the Russian interpreter.

"If you had a magic wand and could wave it to change one thing, only one thing, what would it be?"

As the children replied, I watched the interpreter's face change. She gulped. Tears began to well in her eyes. As she began, hesitantly, to translate their reply for me, her tears began to flow. Mine started too.

It was 1999. I was visiting an orphanage in Tajikistan. I was there to help a Christian relief agency assess the level of need. The mountainous, landlocked country gained independence with the collapse of the Soviet bloc in 1991. After a period of turbulence and civil war, the government was reconstructing essential services with the help of development agencies. Many children had been orphaned or displaced during the fighting. In addition, there were "social orphans," children who had been abandoned by their parents or whose families could not afford to keep them. There were also disabled and vulnerable children living in state-run institutions or international schools run by unqualified, inexperienced childcare workers and some expatriate aid workers.

As a predominantly Muslim country, Tajikistan drew assistance from across the Islamic world, but also from other faith-based agencies with the necessary experience and expertise. I was in the capital Dushanbe with

1. "SFAC—Mick's Story," video at sfac.org.uk, published online March 6, 2010.

48

Chrish Jayasuriya,[2] a young British Sri Lankan aid worker. The city had several large orphanages dating from the Soviet era, some with many hundreds of children. We asked for permission to visit some of these institutions with an interpreter to talk to the children and hear their own views. I much prefer to hear things for myself, to make an informed assessment rather than impose my own ideas or make large-scale assumptions.

The orphanage was gray and rambling, conditions basic. Worse, as was often the case in former Soviet territories or satellite states, there was that all-pervasive air of drabness and gloom. You could almost taste it. There were over 560 children in this single orphanage aged between seven and fourteen. Salaries were insufficient and the orphanage was understaffed. Children were helping with the chores and undertaking additional domestic duties to make up for the lack of support. Inflation ran at 500 percent. The Tajik authorities were finding it difficult to cope. Princess Alice Drive housed 120 children when we arrived and numbers had declined to seventy or eighty by the time we left. By UK standards this orphanage was immense. Not only that, but when I visited another enormous orphanage a two-hour drive away, I found it completely empty. It was like a fortress with heavy gates and thick walls. Yet not a child to be seen.

"Where are the children?" I asked.

"They've all gone home," came the reply.

This was not the last time I saw with my own eyes what the world came increasingly to learn. Many of these "orphanages" were not really orphanages at all. The children had parents, families, homes. These were not orphanages but boarding schools. The children were there to relieve pressure on their families; to be clothed, fed, given an education. It was one thing to find street children or abandoned children in an orphanage, quite another to find children who had homes and families. I was appalled. The whole thing felt so very, very wrong. People are as shocked and surprised as I was when they first hear that the majority of children in residential care have living parents or other close relatives.[3]

2. Now Chrish Erkel.

3. A figure of 80 percent is often cited, particularly by Lumos, a charity led by J. K. Rowling with similar aims to SFAC and other care reform NGOs (Lumos, "Children in Orphanages," lines 1–3). The figure derives from statistics cited in a Save the Children report from 2009 (Csáky, *Keeping Children*). The Politifact website concludes that the figure is based on "credible sources" but some of these are "outdated and, to some extent, unreliable" (Qui, "J.K. Rowling's Charity," lines 8–9). There are also considerable regional variations. Politifact suggests that the highest level based on UNICEF and Better Care

At the enormous orphanage, I organized the children into three groups of three according to age range. With the Russian interpreter, we approached each group in turn.

I asked each group some general questions. What was it like in the orphanage?

"Yes, we have plenty of friends," they told us. "We have food, clothing and education."

I asked them how often they saw their parents.

"Not very often," the children replied.

I then moved up to the older children and asked them, "How long have you been here?"

Some had been there two years, some five years.

I asked them, "Do you know why you are living here?"

They said, "Yes, it's because of poverty. Our parents can't afford to send us to school so they put us into this institution so we will get educated here."

"But you are living away from your family."

"Yes, but it's not that bad. We have lots of food, we have lots of friends, as you can see. We play football, we play basketball. We do lots of things."

Whether they didn't want me to know they were unhappy, I don't know, but they all gave me similar answers.

I moved on to the oldest group, the teenagers, and asked them the same kind of questions through the Russian interpreter. I asked them if they were happy there and they all nodded. I asked them if they wanted to change anything and they said, "No, not really."

Then I said, "Well, okay, let's just imagine this. Let's imagine that you had a magic wand and you could wave that magic wand and have any wish that you mentioned. What would it be?"

They thought for a moment and answered the interpreter in Russian. It was then she started to cry.

"What have they just said?" I asked.

Even though I'd not understood a word, I had anticipated what they might say. I waited for the translation.

"I can't believe what they have just told me," she replied. "They said, 'If I could change just one thing, it would be this. I want a mother or a father.'"

Network reports show 77 percent of 11,000 children in Cambodian orphanages in 2009 having at least one living parent and 90 percent in Sri Lanka in 2007. At the lower end, in Zimbabwe, 39 percent of children in orphanages had at least one living parent (lines 29–33).

I steeled myself to ask my next question. If this was not possible, perhaps if they were orphaned, unwanted, or their parents could not be traced, then would they be happy with a substitute mother or father? They all nodded. They all said, "Yes."

Curious, I asked why that was.

"We want to be like every other child who has a mother and father."

I fought back my tears and thought, "Is *that* what is so important to these children? They want a mother and father more than anything else, but no one has ever asked them."

It struck me more forcibly then than at any time before or since. What children really need is someone just for them. It's not the activities or the entertainment. They want to belong to *someone* and not *something*, a group or organization.

Yes, they had friends. They had a little attention. What they didn't have in an institution was someone of their own.

What you get in an institution is, "Let's do this, let's do that." The system always tries to refocus the child's attention onto something that will take away the inner pain and hurt that they are feeling.

We all need to be loved and to belong. There are millions and millions of children out there who have been abused, messed around, ignored. The place they need to be is in a family, where they are loved and protected and cared for. They do not belong in an institution where they are just a number, one of many.

That incident in Tajikistan taught me so much. I had been a social worker for many years. I knew all the theory—all the influences on child development and behavior. I had even been to Brazil to train social workers, to address conferences of magistrates and academics. I had advocated, lobbied, lectured. I had knocked on doors, rang offices, approached government departments and NGOs. Yet it was this encounter that opened my eyes to what I had already both believed and proclaimed: that children belong in families.

One of the questions I am often asked is why I do what I do.

I refer to this one visit to one orphanage in Tajikistan. It might equally have been in Uganda, or Cambodia, Latin America, or Eastern Europe. The principles are universal. The effect would have been the same.

If you spoke to the trustees of my charity, they would all tell you that Tajikistan was the turning point. Something about that visit galvanized me, gave impetus to the work I had started in Brazil the year before.

Isa Guará opened lots of doors for me in Brazil when we returned early in 1998. By the time we returned to the UK in June, I had addressed dozens of meetings, spoken with hundreds of people, in government, the judiciary, and in social services. They all wanted to hear about foster care. They were all convinced it could work in Brazil. But where was the follow-through? Where was the action? I had begun to lose heart. Everyone I met agreed with me. They were saying the right things. Bringing them to reality was quite another issue. Raising awareness and creating an appetite was one thing. Where was the infrastructure to support family-based care? Even if some within the judiciary were increasingly convinced that fostering was more appropriate than institutional care, how could foster parents be trained, supported, and resourced? People were listening, but that was as far as it seemed to go. I loved Brazil. I loved its color and vibrancy, the warmth and variety. Everywhere I went people told me that they liked what they heard. They were professional, intelligent, engaged. Yet nothing seemed to happen. Nothing seemed to change. Nada.

I was getting very, very frustrated. I had almost given up. What was the point? It was costing me an arm and a leg, so much time and effort and for what? Looking back now, I realize that seeds had been sown. The Brazilians took this message very seriously indeed and were trying to see how it could fit into their systems. It just needed time for it to take root. For myself, it was a time of uncertainty. Where to focus my efforts? Should I concentrate on Latin America or begin to look for opportunities elsewhere?

Meanwhile, the brutal conflict in the Balkans had flared up once more. After the ceasefire of 1995 renewed fighting broke out in 1999. I was back working with Leeds City Council but desperate to do something to help. I rang Tearfund, one of the UK's best-known Christian aid and development agencies. "Look, I'm a social worker, I've done international development, overseas work, children and families. I wondered whether you could use me in some way? Perhaps I could get involved in the Balkans, tracing families, looking to reunite children with their parents or wider family."

They told me that they weren't doing anything of that kind in the Balkans but were involved in other forms of relief. They did know of another organization I might approach. The Christian Outreach Relief and Development (CORD), based in Warwickshire.

I wrote to CORD with an outline of my skills and experience, asking if they could use me in some way. I received an almost immediate response from their development officer. He said, "I can't believe this. Your letter arrived the same day as one asking if I knew someone with your particular skills and experience to assist with a project in Central Asia."

He invited me to Warwickshire to meet Chrish, who had written the request for help. Chrish explained that they were looking to develop family-based care in Tajikistan with government and NGO contacts there. We discussed the scope and details for two or three hours and agreed to get together with the directors to put forward detailed proposals.

A few weeks later, sat in the office of one of the development officers, I mentioned my work in Brazil.

"Oh, that's interesting," he said. "I've been to Brazil."

"Really? Whereabouts was that and what were you doing there?"

We were still discussing Brazil when Chrish came back into the office.

"Run it by me again," she said. "What happened in Brazil to get this whole thing going?"

So I told them about our time working in the children's home and of my encounter with this mysterious guy who had called up to me unexpectedly as I was looking out over the parking lot.

"Well, what did he say then?"

"Not a lot, initially," I replied. "Save to challenge me on some of my cultural attitudes. But he did pray with us and met up with us later to hear what we were doing and then invited us to meet Baroness Cox the next day. He told us his name, but it took us a while to get that out of him!"

"What was his name?" Chrish asked.

When I told her, she smiled and disappeared out of the office.

She returned a few minutes later and said, "Mick, come here."

I followed her out into the corridor and into another office, not sure what to expect. There was Sam, sat at his desk.

He looked up and said, "What are you doing here?"

"Well, what are *you* doing here?" I asked.

"I work here. What are *you* doing here?"

"I'm trying to do what you and Baroness Cox advised us to do. I've been trying to get foster care off the ground in Brazil, but somehow it looks like I've finished up in Central Asia!"

"This is extraordinary," he said. "I rarely work from the office. I'm out and about, I work from a laptop in between meetings, but today I've come in to sort out a few things and in you come!"

I was gobsmacked. I could have easily entered the building, had the meeting, and left without realizing that Sam was there at all. It was only Chrish overhearing my conversation about Brazil by chance that I told the story and that Sam was mentioned at all.

Sam was delighted to see me again and thrilled to hear that Brenda and I had been back to Brazil and how I had begun to engage with government and the judiciary. He was pleased with the prospect of my potential involvement with the project in Tajikistan.

"Keep on going," he said. "Keep on with it."

I rang Brenda after I left the building.

"I don't know what it is, I don't know what's happening, but we're on track. I just know we are on track."

I took the chance meeting with Sam as confirmation that we were now on the right lines. He had been the catalyst. Prior to that, the trips to Romania, the work in the children's home in Brazil, we had been rudderless, working ad hoc, hoping for the best. The way had become clearer, along a very unconventional career path, grammar school to miner to Bible college to residential social worker. At least now I was beginning to apply my professional training, although I still felt hazy about the direction. The second encounter with Sam convinced me we were on track even though I had yet to realize the form our work would take. I've not met Sam since although we have spoken by phone. The Baroness Cox connection was there, though in the background. I didn't know at the time, but Baroness Cox had helped initiate foster care programs in the former Soviet Union.[4] I knew the consultants who had helped her prepare her approach. Other aid and relief agencies had taken encouragement from the success of this program. If it could be done in Russia with its economic problems at that time, it could be done elsewhere.

My second chance encounter with Sam and the impact of the visit to Tajikistan was the spur I needed. I had to see things through.

Almaty International Airport, Kazakhstan. Chrish and I have flown in from Dushanbe for our connecting flight to Frankfurt and from there on home. At passport control, an official examines our documents. He shakes his head. There is a problem. He waves us out of the line and sends for his supervisor. In my mind, I'm back at the border between Paraguay and Brazil. What's wrong this time? Our connecting flight leaves shortly. Miss

---

4. Boyd, *A Voice for the Voiceless*, 94–99, 103–13.

that and I miss my son's wedding at the weekend, stranded in an airport lounge in Kazakhstan. I feel mounting panic as the supervisor explains. We cannot simply pass through Kazakhstan. We need a seventy-two-hour visa. No visa, no flight. I'm stunned. I can see our British Airways plane out on the runway, the passengers heading for the departure lounge.

My suitcase comes off the plane. I see it brought back to the airport lounge and with it all hope of getting out of the country in time. I'm going to miss Mark's wedding.

Mark organized an extended stag party in London, a three-day spree for male relatives and friends. It culminated in a night at the famous Jongleurs Comedy Club. I had coordinated my trip to meet with Chrish and her colleagues so that I could head to London afterward to catch up with Mark at Jongleurs. I then coordinated my return trip from Tajikistan to coincide with the wedding itself. I was cutting it a bit fine, but I figured we could do it. All the connections seemed to tie up neatly, provided nothing went wrong. I hadn't reckoned on the visa issue in Kazakhstan. Apparently, the visas were there, waiting for us in an office. We just hadn't been to collect them. Nothing we could say to assure the airport officials that all was in hand seemed to have any effect. They were not letting us through and that was that.

Chrish remembers me pacing up and down, watching the airport clock as if I could stare time backward.[5] I was praying, I was churning inside, I was desperate. As Chrish was praying too and wondering what to do, an official sidled up to her and gave her a nudge. The passport control officer might take a different view, she suggested, if our passports were "greased" in some way. Chrish took a hundred-dollar bill, inserted it into the passport, and handed it to the officer. He looked, removed the bank note, nodded and let us through.

The passengers had already boarded, the ground crew was clearing the runway ready for take-off. We sped across the tarmac in a little bus with my suitcase, half expecting, even then, for the plane to start to taxi away without us. It was a short distance but it seemed like an age. My heart was pounding, my brain in a whir. We boarded the plane with just minutes to spare. Chrish remembers me sat on the plane in total shock. I was white. "We made it," I kept saying. "We made it . . ."

5. Chrish Erkel, in discussion with Philip Williams, February 9, 2018.

I was to have many more flights, many more near misses. I'd already been delayed from one of my earlier Romanian trips. I took unpaid leave and returned to work later than planned. Valerie was very philosophical and very supportive. She was to get used to me using my vacation time or taking unpaid leave to go hither and yon.

> To me, Mick was something like a missionary, he had this drive and he was very much an individual. He certainly wasn't a saint. He was just an ordinary guy, a fun guy, but very committed. It's been remarkable what his charity has achieved. He would be the first to acknowledge that it's been achieved with the help of other people. Working for a large organization like Leeds City Council will give you professional skills. What it won't do is teach you how to establish and run a charity. Those are the sort of skills picked up by people who run small organizations and I guess Mick had contacts and friends who could help with that. So it's been a joint effort and Brenda's been just as remarkable putting up with it all![6]

Valerie is right. What Leeds City Council provided was a template and a framework. The models we deployed as part of a large municipal authority needed to be adapted if they were to work elsewhere—in different cultures and societies, with different organizations such as charities and NGOs. But as frameworks and structures they were robust. We simply needed to apply them in a more flexible way according to the conditions we encountered around the world. Valerie deserves some extra credit too. She helped develop some of the training materials we used in the early days for potential foster parents. She also gave me time. Not every boss would have done that. Once again, I received the support and encouragement I needed from the right person in the right place at the right time.

My mother died in 2000. To this day, Brenda becomes tearful when she remembers the way Mam came to see us off at the airport when we flew out to Brazil in 1997. We were going for a year but were open to the possibility of staying longer if things worked out and the opportunity arose. Mam was elderly and sometimes ill. There was always the chance that we would not see her again. She came out to visit us when we worked in the children's home. She loved the kids and even went to speak at women's meetings in some of the churches around about, something she had never done before. Not long after she died we moved to another church. It was a lively, charismatic

6. Hales, discussion.

one, as before, and our boys had already become involved there. One Sunday morning, during the service, the pastor broke off preaching to address us directly. For those unused to these things it may sound strange, but, in churches of this kind, it is not unusual for someone to share something they believe to be a message from God or a word of encouragement for someone present. Sometimes these things sound very general. This was different. It was direct and specific.

"Mick and Brenda, I believe God is saying that all the plans you have been waiting for will happen, you will find people drawing alongside you to help bring it to fruition, and what's more, someone is going to pay you to do it!"

We were completely taken aback. What was all this about? Some days later, I went to see the pastor in his office. I told him about our passion, our concern for abandoned and vulnerable children.

"Great," he said. "Then have you thought about starting a charity? You could set up a charity to channel funds and resources to meet this need."

"What? Me?" I responded. "I wouldn't know where to start. I don't know the legal side of it. I wouldn't know how to go about recruiting trustees. I'm not that kind of social worker, I'm not 'political', not an organizer in that sense."

It was like my encounter with Baroness Cox and Sam. I'd been presented with something I had never even considered before. The idea of setting up and heading an organization wasn't even on my radar! I'd already begun to provide consultancy and advice to governments and NGOs, but now I was being asked to set up a charity. I wouldn't even know where to start!

"I know about the process as I've had to do it when setting things in place for the church," our pastor said. "But do you know someone who can help you draft the deeds, the aims and objectives, the core values?"

I did know someone, as it happened, who had written up the deeds for a number of charities. I approached him and explained what I wanted to do and he agreed to draft the deeds for a very reasonable fee. I was clear about the objectives, but I had no idea how to word them for official purposes.

"It's all about getting children into safe, secure families rather than them languishing in children's homes," I said. "How do you get that on paper? How do you write that down?"

We wrote it down. The deeds we drafted then still stand. One of the core objectives is to develop fostering projects for abandoned children in Brazil and other developing countries. This has three subclauses: To provide family and child support services within local communities; Financially assist children's homes and older children with educational fees and/or vocational training; Any other activity that is charitable by law and that would aid the relief of hardship and poverty to children.[7]

It may seem strange to find a reference to children's homes among the objectives we set at that time. After all, wasn't the whole point to find family-based alternatives to institutional care? That objective was enshrined in the name we gave our charity, Substitute Families for Abandoned Children (SFAC). Some years later we changed the name to Strengthening Families for Abandoned Children. Finding a child's original family or a foster family was one thing but supporting them and ensuring they offered safe and secure homes was crucial. To our original lobbying, advocacy, and training, we added a whole range of support measures to help families and communities keep their children at home.

Brenda and I had supported a children's home near São Paulo since our year in Brazil. We recognized that you cannot take a street child, one who might have been involved with drugs or sexual exploitation and place them directly into someone's front room. There had to be an interim stage. Residential care was a temporary measure until such time as the child could return to their biological family or be placed with appropriate foster parents or an adoptive family.

The pastor's advice was very wise and helped us immeasurably later on. He recommended that we worded the trust documents in such a way that I could be both director and employed either full-time or part-time at some point in the future. He was convinced that I would one day work full-time in the charity, far more convinced than I was. For three years I juggled running the charity with my full-time job at Leeds City Council. In 2005 I went freelance, taking on casework for various local authorities to support my charitable work. In 2010, thanks to the generosity of a major supporter, I was able to work part-time for the charity. Eventually I went full-time. But all that lay in the future. For now, our objectives were set. The deeds signed. All we needed now were donors and supporters.

7. Declaration of Trust, Substitute Families for Abandoned Children, August 29, 2002.

6. Moving Forward

WE HAD TO BE PATIENT. WE HAD TO PERSIST.
WE HAD TO SEE IT THROUGH.

BEEP BEEP BIP BEEP beep!

The connection slowly blinked to life and the world began to drip and download onto the old PC. These were still the days of dial-up. If we were lucky, we had around half an hour each evening to email friends and family.

As I waited for the connection I thought of my pay phone calls to John Ellerington when I was at my lowest ebb in Birmingham. I pressed the coins into the slot at the appointed weekly time. A hundred miles north he awaited my call in a red telephone kiosk, once such an iconic feature of the British streetscape. Now, technology had moved on. We had the internet. From a mission station and children's home in Brazil, we could send messages to family and friends back home.

Or we could, in between power cuts and lost connections, or if those at the receiving end *had* computers. John did not. Fortunately, his friends Tony and Vivienne Hodges did. We sent a weekly email to Tony who printed it off for John so he could pass news on to our families. To this day, Tony is embarrassed to admit that he would read those emails. He was intrigued. Who was this couple that John and Jane Ellerington knew in Brazil? What were they doing there? Every Sunday evening his 28.8 kbit modem flickered and bleeped as another message came in for John. He would print the email out, trying not to read the contents, but something would catch his eye. Guiltily, he would take a peek.

We first met Tony and Vivienne at Christmas 1997 as we were waiting to renew our visas to return to Brazil. John and Jane suggested that we meet up with them for a meal. They had expressed interest in the work we were doing and wanted to know more. We told them about our time in Brazil, how we had to leave the country, our chance meeting with Sam and Baroness Cox, and how we planned to return.

Tony and Vivienne ran a small but successful pensions and employee benefits consultancy. Back then, the company was in its infancy. It now has offices in the UK, Australia, and the US. They knew John and Jane through an Anglican church they attended in a small town near Wakefield. Both were interested in supporting charities. Vivienne had been a long-standing supporter of a children's home in Uganda. It was based on a farm model, with children living in groups. I had seen similar arrangements in Brazil and was to work with people who ran such schemes. To my mind, they were better than traditional, drab, cold orphanages, but still less than ideal. Vivienne was surprised. Surely the children were cared for? They had plenty of friends and warm human contact. The farm taught them valuable skills. They had fresh air, food, and exercise. All these things are true of course, and as an interim solution between residential and family-based care, such schemes have their place. They lack that central ingredient though, the one so powerfully expressed by the children in Tajikistan. They lack *attachment*. In the "children's village" model then popular in many African countries, the children each share a care provider. These are usually female, single, and with children of their own which they often leave in the care of relatives while they work away from home. They often travel long distances, breaking up their own family in the process. It is a system that can be counterproductive. It separates families. In Uganda and other African countries, the government discourages this particular model for these reasons.[1]

Vivienne had seen the appalling conditions in some African orphanages for herself. She was satisfied that farm models offered a better solution. When she heard my contention that family-based care was the ideal, she immediately agreed. The attachment issue clinched it for her. Her only concern was the potential timescale.

"Surely it will take you ages to work that out," she said. "One child at a time, one by one, finding suitable families, vetting them, making sure they are the right home. The farm system may not be ideal, but at least it can handle groups of children at the same time."[2]

---

1. From the author's direct field observations and Joseph Luganda (programmes manager, CALM Africa), in discussion with Philip Williams, May 30, 2018.

2. Tony and Vivienne Hodges, in discussion with Philip Williams, February 15, 2018.

I agreed. It would take a long time. But it had to happen. There was a better way. We had to work toward family-based care, however long it took. Children belong in families.

We kept in touch with the Hodges. In 2002, as SFAC came into being, Tony flew out with me to Brazil to see the work in the children's home we supported. We had met Pedrinho and Noemi da Silva Neto during our interrupted year in Brazil. We supported them from 1998 as they took street children into their home. I always saw it as an interim solution. Until fostering gained traction in Brazil, residential care and adoption remained the only long-term options for these children. A "group home" like this one gave children a caring environment until alternatives developed. I knew this would be a matter of time. We had to be patient. We had to persist. We had to see it through.

You learn a lot about people when you travel with them. With Tony, I learned what good fun he could be and saw his genuine compassion for the downtrodden and the underdog. I also found out how loudly he snored! I learned that he was under strict instructions, as he put it, not to commit to any support until he had evaluated everything and, quite rightly, discussed it with Vivienne at home. They might be visionary entrepreneurs, but they had sound common sense and were not going to support anything until they had evaluated it properly.

Tony came with me to the children's home. He asked questions, left no stone unturned. One evening we sat down for a meal with some of the aid workers. As Tony recounts it he suddenly felt a burning conviction, quite out of the blue, to support the work. He could only describe it as something he took to be a "prompting" from the Holy Spirit.[3] Even though he had agreed to wait until he returned to the UK he felt a sudden compunction to help fund the work there and then.

To everyone's surprise, he announced his intention. To this day I don't know which of us was the more amazed; Tony, the Brazilian aid workers, the interpreter, or me. After Tony made his announcement one of the Brazilians quoted a verse from the Book of Proverbs in the Old Testament. Tony says that before I gave the English translation, he already knew which verse the aid worker had quoted: "It is the blessing of the Lord that makes rich. And he adds no sorrow to it."[4] The verse had particular resonance for

3. T. and V. Hodges, discussion.
4. Prov 10:22 NASB.

Tony. The vicar quoted it when he and Vivienne married. He remembered it carrying a particular weight and quality which stayed with him. To hear it again, in this different context, made a powerful impression.

The support Tony and Vivienne gave us made a substantial difference. It still does. We often joke about those times when he cast furtive, glances at our emails to John Ellerington. Are we glad he did! Yet another person was in the right place at the right time! Other donors came on board, friends and family, through church and through our trustees. We picked up some early donors from a broadcast on one of the UK's first Christian TV channels. A number of people who had also known us over the years also pledged amounts from £5 ($7) a month. One faithful young man continues to support us to the tune of £1 ($1.4) a month, a small but regular amount and gratefully received. Gradually we built up some financial stability for the charity.

Times were tough during the early 1980s. Unemployment was high. Life was hard for many of our friends in Leeds. At one time it seemed that most were unemployed or working in commission-only jobs as driving instructors or insurance salesmen. By the end of the decade, the economy had picked up. Most of our friends were in full-time work or self-employed. Andrew Grimshaw, who instigated our trips to Romania, was running his own chiropody practice. He told one of his patients about our work and she immediately offered to help with our accounts. Jean was retired but had many years' experience keeping the accounts for another NGO. Her help in preparing end-of-year reports was invaluable.

I received invitations to speak at women's midweek fellowship meetings at various churches. I had to squeeze some of these into my lunch hour when working for Leeds City Council! We often received small donations. The bulk of our funding came from our network of contacts and the freelance contract work I carried out for local authorities.

By 2006 I had returned to Brazil several times and visited Tajikistan. Opportunities opened up in Colombia and other countries. As a childcare and child protection specialist, I was very aware of the work carried out by foster agencies. I had also noticed how plush some of their offices were, the kinds of cars the directors drove. They clearly weren't short of money. Perhaps I could approach some of these private companies for support?

Independent foster agencies grew up alongside the local government systems, either to provide specialist services or to meet rising demand.

Typically, in the UK, the local government authority recruited foster parents who were paid an allowance to cover their expenses.

As the pressure grew on local authority budgets, independent agencies developed to meet demand. They recruited and paid foster parents and sometimes offer specialist services, such as additional support for mental health and disabilities.

I worked with several of these agencies during my local authority career. I knew how they worked, the kind of services they offered. I looked online and found perhaps sixty-five agencies that looked promising. I wrote to them explaining what I was doing and inviting them to contact me. I was convinced that this was my passport to finance for the charity. It seemed so obvious. If you were making money in the UK to see children raised in foster families, then surely, you could spare a little of that to support exactly the same kind of work overseas?

I was staggered by the lack of response. It hurt and shocked me. I knew for a fact that there were foster agency directors who were multimillionaires. At that time, it was possible to make a lot of money running a foster agency, less so now due to increased competition. I received about three or four responses. Friends who work in marketing tell me this is a reasonable return on an initial piece of unsolicited direct mail. But I was surprised. I had expected more to at least hear me out. But among these responses was one from someone I hadn't even written to. Walter Young. I wrote to his codirector at Team Fostering, one of the few not-for-profit fostering agencies in the UK. The codirector passed it on to Walter saying, "This is more your thing. Big picture stuff."

Walter rang me and said, "I like the sound of what you are doing. Can I come and see you?"

"What, here?"

"Yes, I'd like to come and see you in your office."

I worked from a bedroom tabletop at that time. Since then we have built an extension with office space.

"I work from one of the bedrooms," I blurted, rather embarrassed at the thought of him coming to the house. "Are you sure it wouldn't be better for me to come up to you?"

"No, no, it's fine," said Walter. "We have an office in Sheffield, I can easily pop in to see you in Leeds, have a chat, and then go on to a meeting there."

Team Fostering is based in Newcastle-upon-Tyne, around a hundred miles north of Leeds. It seemed a long way for Walter to come, but I agreed.

The other responses were encouraging and friendly but offered no support. One agency had only recently formed links with a charity working in Belarus. Another had made a similar arrangement elsewhere. At least they were doing something, even if it wasn't with us. Walter, it seemed, was our only hope. He was a godsend, completely committed to what we do. He brought something extra from his private sector practice to add to my own local authority experience. Walter has a degree in psychology as well as in social work, he is entrepreneurial, has business acumen and a strategic approach. He also believes in what we are doing. It was a combination that proved invaluable.

Walter sits in our front room. I offer him a cup of Colombian coffee.

"So, tell me what you are doing and why you do it? How you do it?"

I answer him as honestly and straightforwardly as I can.

"Can you show me some of what you do?" he asks.

"I certainly can, Walter. But it's on my computer up in the spare bedroom."

I feel very self-conscious. Here is one of the directors of a private fostering agency and we are running a charity from a computer in a bedroom. Walter is very gracious. He doesn't seem fazed at all. He simply asks questions and then gets up to leave.

"So you're off to Sheffield now?" I ask him on the doorstep.

"No, I'm heading back up to Newcastle, the Sheffield meeting was canceled."

It is then I realize we had struck a chord. He had come all the way down from Newcastle simply to see me. Something must have resonated for him to do that without another meeting to attend.

When we next spoke on the phone he said, "The Internet is a wonderful thing, Mick. People can put anything online. It looks the part, it looks convincing, but it may not bear any relation to reality. I had to come down to see you to judge for myself. I'm going to present something to the board and see what the other directors make of it."

Within a few weeks, Walter contacted me again. His company would support us with a fixed sum a month. He also asked if he could come with me on my planned trip to Colombia. I was delighted. Until that time I had done everything on my own. It was hard work. It *is* hard work. It isn't just the fieldwork and the sessions with the social workers and prospective foster parents. It is everything that goes with international travel, booking flights, hotels, sorting visas and paperwork, cultural adjustments, making contingency plans.

People think that working abroad and visiting exotic places is a "jolly."[5] It isn't. When you fly into another country people expect things from you and what they expect is very often those things you are struggling with. Simply by virtue of your being there, they think you are the expert, the person with all the answers. They assume you have some magic wand or some secret source of funding, the key that will unlock every solution. It's not just holding and conveying the information. It's the pressure of making it all work and your involvement as effective and interesting as possible. You have to be on the ball, you have to turn up as expected and where expected and you have to deliver. You have to be on top of your game, even if you're feeling unwell. It is physically and emotionally draining. When you have done a week's work, through an interpreter most of the time, when you are introducing concepts people might be unfamiliar with and you want to ensure they understand, it takes it out of you. It is hard, hard work, particularly when you are on your own. So the prospect of having Walter with me on my next trip was like manna from heaven.

The only concern I had was how he would perform. Walter sent me copies of the slides for his presentation. There were charts, graphs, facts, figures, strategic curves. I sent them back and asked him to redo them. Now it was his turn to be out of his comfort zone.

"We are talking to social workers, aren't we?"

"Yes, some of them will be. But we'll also be addressing general aid workers, missionaries, government officials."

"They've been to university, haven't they?"

"Well, some of them, but even if they have, it's too technical. This stuff will be new to most of them. We need to keep it practical."

I sent the revised slides off for translation. While I was waiting for them to come back Walter asked, "Do you mind if my wife comes with us?"

"Here we go," I thought. "Strings attached!" I had never met Walter's wife, but it turned out she was another director in the company and also a social worker. I admit I was worried. I was used to being a one-man band. It was hard work on my own, but at least I had some semblance of control. I had a four-day residential in Colombia for social workers and government officials. How would these new people perform? I had no need to worry.

5. British rhyming colloquialism for holiday or vacation.

Elaine Young was brilliant. So was Walter. They both went down a storm. The conference delegates loved them. The kids we visited loved them too. It was a truly memorable trip.

We visited several children's homes, all highly secured behind bars and gates. We were told that the gates were less to keep intruders out but the children in. These were ten-year-old kids, not teenagers, but they were on glue or other drugs. If they ever slipped out of the homes, they would disappear back onto the streets. If the security was tight on the outside, there was very little privacy inside. We were shown to our rooms, trundling our luggage across echoing tiles. There were no doors so that supervisors could keep an eye on the kids at all times. These were street kids. What happened on the streets would happen in the home. I felt awkward. Here I was, with the sponsors of the trip, and I had led them to a place where they had to sleep on bunk beds with me in the next room, no door, and behind a paper-thin wall. We would call out to each other in the night.

"Are you alright, Walter?" "Are you settling down, Elaine?" "How are you doing, Mick?"

We may as well have all been in the same room.

We have often laughed about our experiences on that first trip and the Youngs have been part of what we have been doing ever since.

Walter's involvement marked another stage in the development of SFAC. Up until that point we had relied on personal contacts. John Ellerington remembers my inviting him to a trailer up in the Yorkshire Dales to discuss this idea I had. We had sold our trailer home in the Midlands but had access to one in Yorkshire, where I would sometimes go to plan, pray, and think things through. I knew John loved walking in the countryside. I figured that he may hear me out and perhaps offer some help if I outlined my ideas in that context.

John found it very cloak-and-dagger, all very mysterious.[6] He said it took him a while to "clock" what I was talking about. John was always quite creative and arty. He had gone into art dealing once he left school, but later, despite the hours spent on the public pay phone listening to my woes, he too went into social work. He too worked in childcare and knew the fostering and adoption system very well. He was one of our original trustees and

---

6. John Ellerington, SFAC trustees in discussion with Philip Williams, November 14, 2017.

remained so for many years. He accompanied me on some of my trips to Brazil and was amazed at the sizes of the audiences we addressed.

"There we were in these vast auditoria. Upward of 500 people, judges, magistrates, social workers, government officials, I was stunned. How had this happened? We are just two blokes from Knottingley. How come we're addressing people at this level?"[7]

We had met Tony and Vivienne through John and Jane. Now, with the Team Fostering link with Walter and Elaine, we were moving beyond our immediate contacts and beyond the church and Christian context.

Walter remembers receiving my letter.

> For most of my social work career I worked in fostering, firstly in a local authority fostering service and then in the independent sector. My views of family-based care were influenced by working in residential care and seeing how children do much better in families. The majority of children and young people deserve to be in a family and actually can be placed in a family and have much better outcomes than in an institution. So that's very much been at the core of my values and my reason for working in this field. So when Mick's letter arrived I was quite intrigued by it, because it was clearly written by somebody whose values were in alignment with my own but working in developing countries. With hindsight, I wish I had kept the letter, but I remember how it got me interested because it pointed out how large numbers of children were in institutional care and how there are people working to support governments and NGOs who want to place children into families. So it really hit home in terms of what I believe in and what I think is best for children. It showed me how someone was trying to do in other parts of the world what we were trying to promote back home.
>
> It was very clear from the letter that it was a Christian organization and I'm not a Christian myself, but I felt that was secondary in a way. Obviously, their faith was very much a big part of what motivates them to do it, but for me, it was a pragmatic view in that I can work with people within all sorts of belief systems, even though I don't hold to them myself. I thought that perhaps this was an organization we could work with. So I contacted him and arranged to meet him in his home, where he was working before he had the office set up. I remember drinking some coffee he brought back from Colombia and thinking, 'Wow! Colombia, wouldn't that be something!' I also remember being very impressed by

7. Ibid.

how Mick was going about this work. I've always been someone who admires people who are practical, pragmatic, and who get things done. It struck me that Mick was doing what he did very effectively.[8]

Walter has worked with us in many countries and across different cultures. He has accompanied me on training visits to Uganda, Southeast Asia, Ethiopia, Colombia, Morocco, and Iraq. He has seen how the principles we both hold can and do work in Islamic cultures, Christian cultures, largely Buddhist cultures, or where there is no one dominant faith tradition. From the outset, we wanted to work across boundaries of culture and creed. The best interests of the child lie at the heart of all we do. The shape that takes and the way it might be administered may vary from country to country, but essentially the principles are transferable and universal.

When I explain to people what we do the reaction is almost invariably the same.

"That's a no-brainer! It's so obvious! Of course, children belong in families. Why can't everyone see that?"

I smile to myself and think, "If only you knew. If only you knew the barriers, the excuses, the vested interests on the one hand or the genuine lack of awareness on the other."

Our systems were in place. We had donors and support. We could draw on the expertise of experienced practitioners like Walter and Elaine. Our original trustees, John Ellerington, John Swift, and Andrew Grimshaw were all excellent and competent men. There were openings for us around the world.

There was one more thing we had to do. We had to show that foster care could work in developing countries. We had to show that it could work across all cultures, amid poverty and political turmoil, in the face of vested interests or genuine ignorance. Some of the toughest battles, and also some of our biggest victories, would come from within my own faith tradition.

The battle had begun.

8. Walter Young, in discussion with Philip Williams, January 18, 2018.

7. In the Absence of Love

IN THE ABSENCE OF LOVE, THERE IS NO PAIN IN LOSS.
— VERA FAHLBERG,
A CHILD'S JOURNEY THROUGH PLACEMENT

"WHAT MAKES A GOOD foster family?"

I pitch the question to a missionary conference as part of a session on family-based alternatives to residential care.

"A Christian family," is the immediate response from one of the delegates.

"Okay—but what makes you think that? I know of instances where Christian families have made less than ideal foster parents, or biological parents come to that."

"Someone who doesn't drink."

"Well, I'm partial to a glass of wine now and again. Would that disqualify me from becoming a foster parent?"

"Someone who doesn't smoke," the missionary persists.

I can see I'm going to have a struggle on my hands. As I carry on with my presentation it's the missionary's turn to ask a question. It comes in shocked tones.

"So, tell me, are you saying that it's right for children to be placed with Muslim families, or Hindu families, or families of other religions or with no faith?"

"Yes. That's exactly what I am saying. The key issue is the best interests of the child."

The missionary is horrified. Surely, I am limiting that child's chance to hear and respond to the Gospel? It is an objection I have heard many times from those who see faith-based orphanages primarily as a means to convert children.

I hear mutterings and murmurings across the hall. I repeat my point. The key is the best interests of the child. Is it in a child's best interests to remove them from their culture and community, convert them, and send them back into settings where they may be shunned or even persecuted for their faith? What a terrible position to put a child into, having to make such a stark choice between their culture and community, their family and their faith. The key issue is always the best interests of the child. It's not the best interests of the organization, the churches, workers, or individual supporters that counts. We all need to fall in line behind the best interests of the child. Surely their personal safety is of prime importance? In the training we deliver through SFAC, we often use an exercise in which we list children's needs and ask participants to rank them in order of priority. The list includes education, health, emotional well-being, religion, the opportunity to live with their own or another family and being safe from harm. Participants always rank the options differently and that is fine. There is no right or wrong answer to the priority order apart from the first two, the paramount concerns. The child's safety should always come first and foremost. Next come the child's emotional well-being and sense of belonging or attachment. Once these principal needs are met, the rest can be ranked in any order; education, health, family, religion, and so on.

I remind the missionary group that I firmly believe in the power of the Christian message. I believe it holds the answer to humanity's problems at the deepest level. I also believe that our aim in providing appropriate childcare is not primarily to proselytize or preach. Our role is to ensure that children entrusted to our care receive all the help and support they need. It is their life, their family, their community, their culture. Just imagine how they would feel as adults if they were presented with such stark choices; between newly found faith and family, friends, and community? As an adult, you may decide to make that choice, but we are dealing with extremely isolated and vulnerable children who are in no position to even contemplate the implications of such a decision.

The murmurs turn into nods of assent. They are beginning to get it. The message hits home. First and foremost, a child needs safety. Next, a child needs somewhere to belong. These are not the only things they need, of course. They may need some forms of therapy, help with speech or learning difficulties. They may need psychotherapy or help with movement and motor skills. Whatever other needs they have, all children require love, nurture, and support. The pediatrician and psychologist Vera Fahlberg puts it very clearly.

> All children . . . need love and nurturing from a family. They need a basic sense of safety. Additionally, they need parents to have appropriate expectations for them and to place controls on their behaviors. Finally, they look to their family for role modeling. All children deserve to believe that they are loved. It is the everyday happenings in the child's life which provides this. When the child is hungry, someone feeds him. When she is tired she is tucked in bed. When troubled, he is comforted. She has opportunities to play. These things happen not because the child has been good, but because these things are good for children. Parents initiate many positive interactions, he or she feels worthwhile or loveable. It is precisely when adults and children alike least deserve love that they need it most.[1]

UNICEF estimates that at least 2.7 million children up to seventeen years old live in institutional care worldwide. However, it acknowledges that this is just the tip of the iceberg since many institutions are unregistered and the children in them uncounted.[2] Some put the figure as high as over eight million.[3] The truth is, we don't really know for sure. Many of these institutions are run by churches and mission agencies. In Zimbabwe, of some twenty-four orphanages built between 1996 and 2006, 80 percent of them were established by faith groups with 90 percent of the funding coming from Pentecostal or independent churches.[4] The number of orphanages in Uganda rose from thirty in 1992 to an estimated 800 by 2013.[5] Over 95 percent of these institutions were not appropriately licensed by the Ugandan government.[6] A study in Ghana found that only eight out of 148

---

1. Fahlberg, *A Child's Journey*, 277. Fahlberg's book guides practitioners through the issues of attachment and bonding, child development, separation, and loss. It contains case studies and advice on how to minimize the trauma of transitions and moves.

2. See Petrowski et al., "Number of Children in Formal Alternative Care."

3. Lumos regularly cites this figure. It has been disputed but most sources agree that the UNICEF estimates are conservative.

4. Powell et al., *The Zimbabwean Experience*, vi.

5. Boothby et al., "Effective Early Response Strategies," quoted in Bunkers, *Children, Orphanages*, 5.

6. Riley, "Uganda's Alternative Care Framework," quoted in ibid., 5.

known orphanages were licensed in 2009.[7] Indonesia has more than 8,000 residential institutions housing more than half a million children. In 2009 an astonishing 99 percent of them were run by faith-based organizations and were unregulated.[8]

All this begs important questions. How has this situation come about? Why are many faith-based residential institutions reluctant to register with the appropriate authorities? Are the terms "orphans" and "orphanages" even the right one to use? Christians and people of other faiths are often among the first to respond in emergencies; in times of war, epidemics, and famine. They are often very generous and genuinely keen to alleviate suffering, poverty, and need. I think of my own father, apportioning his often-meager wages to donate to the Leprosy Mission and other agencies. Christians often respond generously and rapidly, but sadly, not always in ways that are properly thought through. Good intentions are not good enough. Some well-meaning attempts to help are amateurish and ill considered. Individuals and organizations can fail to grasp the complexity of the problems. They operate in a "quick fix" or "rescue" mode. We live in a world of twenty-four-hour news coverage and social media. It is a world of "instant response." Set up a crowdfunding group. Sign an online petition. We've done it ourselves. I sprang into a truck with some friends to drive supplies to Romania with good intentions. Some items we thought would help proved completely useless. Brenda and I responded to the shootings of street children in Brazil by parking our jobs to volunteer in a children's home. In neither instance, for all our good intentions, did we consider what might be better alternatives. What we did on an individual level, many faith-based organizations do at an institutional level. They make a well-intentioned but knee-jerk response. They can be naive and uninformed. Their zeal and enthusiasm can often override the need for care and attention, systems and procedures, due process and accountability. We learned from our mistakes; so can organizations and institutions. This is not about pointing fingers. Once we understand the issues we can begin to apply solutions.

Organizations can and do change. What might be true of them at one point in their development may no longer be the case some years on. At one

---

7. According to Helen Obeng Asamoah, assistant director of the Social Welfare Department of Ghana government. See IRIN News, "Protecting Children," lines 5–9, cited in Csáky, *Keeping Children*, 3.

8. Csáky, *Keeping Children*, 19.

time, Barnardo's and NCH in the UK were all about providing residential childcare. They do so no longer. They have evolved into organizations that advocate for children's rights and work to strengthen and support families. The same is true for many faith-based and secular childcare organizations in North America, Europe, Australia, and elsewhere. In most African, South Asian, and Far Eastern countries, long-term residential childcare is comparatively new. It was introduced by missionaries and colonial governments in the nineteenth and early twentieth centuries. They replicated what was then the norm in their home nations. In the immediate postwar period, Western countries began to shift their emphasis from long-term residential care to family-based alternatives such as fostering and adoption. There were strong moves away from children's homes not only in Western Europe and North America but also in the southern cone of South America; Argentina, Chile, Uruguay.[9]

The older Christian churches and denominations such as the Catholics, Anglicans, and Presbyterians also gradually embraced family-based models in our home countries. Yet the number of faith-based residential homes has recently increased across the developing world. A new generation of independent organizations sprang up very rapidly, largely from within the evangelical or Pentecostal constituency. Pentecostals are probably the largest single supporting group of faith-based residential institutions across the world today. Compared to the traditional denominations, their approach is more informal and unregulated. They work largely through relationships formed at grassroots level. It is entrepreneurial and often more closely embedded in local communities, but equally, very volatile. If relationships break down, their work with children often breaks down with it.

There can also be a strong suspicion of official regulations and formal structures, particularly when they are perceived to come from opposing secular sources or other faith traditions. The authorities will interfere if we tell them what we are doing, they say. They might clamp down on our attempts to spread the Gospel. They are secular authorities, they don't understand. Christians are in a minority here, they need our support. The children will find faith here. We are raising up the future indigenous Church, the next generation of pastors and evangelists, even presidents. How often have I heard that statement! Of course, I gently remind them

9. Llorente et al., *Children in Institutions*. Additional observations from Philip Aspegren (executive director of Casa Viva), in discussion with Philip Williams, February 21, 2018.

that the Bible has something to say about complying with the laws of the land, about acting openly and transparently![10] We need to both act within the law and promote good practice.

Sadly, many of these groups currently operate in ways that are no longer in tune with professional consensus and practice. They might be incredibly enterprising and entrepreneurial in the way they run their churches, but they're way behind the times when it comes to running orphanages! Philip Aspegren, executive director of Casa Viva, an NGO in Costa Rica, tells of a Californian megachurch with the very latest in sound systems and lighting, where the pastor delivers sermons from a couch like a TV chat show host. Yet they think nothing of flying to Guatemala, say, and setting up an orphanage that Charles Dickens would have considered old-fashioned![11] I have seen shocking conditions, terrible examples of poor practice, but more often, examples of naivety and a lack of understanding of what children actually need.

I have also seen orphanages used to attract donations that then go toward other initiatives. The orphanage acts as a front to fund another project, a Bible college perhaps. At the extreme, there are even instances of child trafficking from faith-based institutions. Well-meaning Western couples adopt children from residential homes in developing countries, only to find that the child's parents are still alive. All have been cruelly duped.[12] There are well-publicized instances of families who have returned children they have adopted in good faith to their birth mothers, at great cost and heartache to themselves. There is money to be made from running a children's home, money to be made from international adoption. Tragically, the best-intentioned people can often be naive and therefore vulnerable to exploitation.[13]

---

10. There are, of course, a range of understandings within Christian theology on issues of individual conscience and compliance with secular authorities. The issue here is not so much about issues of conscience but compliance with generally accepted national and international standards and even basic codes of practice for child protection and safety. It never ceases to amaze me how people who would be so carefully compliant with regulations in their own country seem so oblivious to standards in someone else's!

11. Aspegren, discussion.

12. Kaye and Drash, "Kids for sale." For a full treatment of this issue within the US evangelical constituency, see Joyce, "The Trouble."

13. For a hard-hitting critique of some US evangelical practices around international adoption and residential childcare, see Joyce, *Child Catchers*. Additional insights on these issues come from discussions with Joseph Luganda and Mark Riley in Uganda.

It comes as a shock when many people discover that some orphanages will often employ "child finders," agents whose job it is to fill their dormitories, to recruit children for their residential institutions. The more children they have in their "orphanages," the more donations they can attract. Let's not forget that orphanage directors have families to feed. Running an institution is their job. Their livelihood depends upon it. No "orphans" means no income. It is a simple equation. They need to attract donors and sponsors to keep their institutions going. They need children to fill their homes. It is easy for those of us in the affluent West to be critical of such people. Yet many orphanage directors come from the poorest backgrounds too. Running an orphanage presents them with an opportunity to earn a living. Those of us who work in care reform need to understand that. It was another lesson I had to learn. What is far less easy to condone or understand are the tactics of unscrupulous operators, many of them from the West or else sponsored by Western-backed orphanages or adoption agencies.

In Uganda, Joseph Luganda from the family support NGO, CALM Africa,[14] can tell you how plausible their recruiters sound. They come armed with glossy brochures, slick presentations, and appealing photographs to overawe and impress their largely illiterate target population. They choose the poorest villages, the most deprived areas. Some offer payment, in cash or in kind, to persuade families to part with their children. It all appears so polished, so plausible. Your child now has the opportunity to be educated, well clothed and well fed. First, they have to move to this distant orphanage. Perhaps they will get a good job in the city, be able to send money home to alleviate your poverty. Just think of the difference this could make to you and your family's future!

The cold reality is that some of these families will never see their children again. They "sign" an ambiguous document they can neither read nor fully understand. At best, they may see their child occasionally if they are able to visit the "orphanage." At worst, their child may disappear, lost to a distant city or even trafficked abroad.[15] It is harrowing, it is distressing, it is wrong. These children have families. Someone needs to find them and, where possible, reunite them.

---

14. CALM Africa is a Ugandan charity focused on the rights and protection of children. It began in 1985 as a self-help group supporting children affected by AIDS. It evolved into a community group and then a registered charity working at a national level. See http://www.calmafrica-ug.org/.

15. Luganda, in discussions with Philip Williams, February 13 and May 30, 2018.

Let's face facts. In many instances, some—but by no means, all—faith-based orphanages contribute to family separation. They may also perpetuate rather than alleviate poverty and deprivation. They separate children from their parents and communities. How ironic when faith groups often espouse the importance of family values. How ironic that to respond to crises involving family breakdown and separation, so many agencies perpetuate a system that does exactly that. They may be doing so innocently and unwittingly, but they are doing it. They add to the problem. One of the things we do at SFAC is help them become part of the solution.

It is yet another of those chance encounters that occur so often in the story of SFAC. Tony Hodges is driving just west of London when his car phone rings. A colleague tells him he is with someone Tony might be interested to meet.

"He's an American who does all sorts of work with kids out in Myanmar and other countries. He seems a really great guy. I'm sure you'd be interested to speak to him while he's in the UK. I don't know how you're fixed—"

"Sure, sounds interesting. Where are you?"

When he hears the location, Tony starts bolt upright in his seat. "Why, that's just a mile from where I'm driving! Would he mind if I came right over?"[16]

David Servant was in the UK meeting trustees of Heaven's Family, the charity he runs from the US. At that time, it was also registered in the UK and had sponsors and supporters there. He was at a house party run by one of his British trustees when Tony turned up. They spoke about David's work in Myanmar sponsoring children in orphanages.

Tony said, "That's really interesting. I have a good friend here who is involved with that kind of thing, only from a different angle. His work involves finding secure homes with families as an alternative to residential care. It's a different take on things, but you may be interested to hear how it works. I can call him on my cell phone if you like."

David agreed and Tony rang me, introduced me to David and we spoke for half an hour. David recalls sitting on the stairs of his trustees' house and listening as I systematically dismantled the entire basis for his work to date!

---

16. T. and V. Hodges, discussion.

Mick was very gentle, very measured. He didn't try to force anything down my throat. He simply gave a synopsis of the work he did and why he felt it offered a better alternative. My heart resonated with what he said, but I realized that if I believed and embraced what Mick was telling me, then it would involve a major change. It would involve us totally rearranging our model.[17]

David tells how he handed the phone back to Tony after our conversation and allowed the thoughts to "percolate." A few months later, I answered the phone and found, to my surprise, David on the line.

"Mick, remember our conversation? We've got to talk."

I hadn't expected this. I had torn into his methodology and now he was back in touch and with a proposal too! David invited me over to Myanmar to address orphanage directors in two cities, representing over forty orphanages in all. He wanted me to outline for them what I had told him about family-based care as an alternative to residential solutions. I accepted his invitation. Since my first conversation with him, David had wrestled with the issues and the implications for the way his charity operated. He had researched the issue further. He became convinced that what I had described was the right way for them to go. What they needed now was training and information on how to make the transition.

David describes the way that children can be exploited in some faith-based orphanages as "hair-raising."[18] Some orphanage directors drill and train the children to worship, sing, and pray on cue, for the benefit of potential sponsors. In some instances, the children are required to pray in unison, often with tears, at the tops of their voices at six in the morning, before they have had their breakfast. They can turn it on and off like the flick of a switch. It's meant to impress donors with the children's spiritual zeal.

I have heard stories of itinerant evangelists who scoop children up off the streets of India and take them over the border to orphanages in Myanmar. There are no questions asked, no audit trail, no records or paperwork. Who will ever know where that child originates from? How will they ever find their way home? These missionaries may be doing this for what they believe to be the right motives, taking the child off the streets—if they were ever truly on the streets in the first place! Yet they take them many hundreds of miles from their community to another country, another language, another culture and abandon them, only to move on themselves and leave

17. David Servant, in discussion with Philip Williams, January 15, 2018.

18. D. Servant, discussion.

no trace. Then, when visitors come from Western countries, the orphanages parade the kids and proclaim that they are training the next generation of indigenous missionaries. Please give generously. Sign this pledge. Set up an account through your church.

It has been going on for years. I've heard of a former Australian missionary who worked in India in the 1980s. On one occasion, an Indian orphanage director, with an empty building, borrowed children from another institution to fill it for the duration of a visit by potential American donors! David Servant puts it bluntly.

> There is an orphanage *industry* in Southeast Asia. It is literally an industry. That is the only term I can use for it, an industry with so many components. They employ recruiters who go around the villages collecting kids to fill their institutions. In the Christianized parts of Myanmar, there are almost as many Bible schools as orphanages. Each feeds off the other. If you are from a poor Christian family in Chin State, you go into an orphanage hundreds of miles away, in Yangon or one of the other large cities. You come out of the orphanage and attend Bible school. When you leave Bible school you set up an orphanage.[19]

It is a self-perpetuating system. The more kids the orphanages get, the more sponsors and donations they can attract. The existence of these homes acts as a pull factor, encouraging poorer families to relinquish care of their own children in the belief that these institutions will provide free food, clothes, and education—a better start in life.[20] Most institutions I've encountered are run by poorly trained volunteers or low paid staff. However better resourced or well-intentioned others might be they are still less than ideal. Traumatized and vulnerable children require far more from their care providers. Residential institutions often offer them far less. The most vulnerable children get the worst possible deal. Sometimes, children are sexually abused, if not by staff then by visitors or other children.[21] More often, however, problems arise from the deployment of unskilled or voluntary labor, well-meaning people with little or no experience of looking after other people's children and the issues these children bring with them.

19. D. Servant, discussion.

20. Ruslan Maliuta (international facilitator, World Without Orphans), in discussion with Philip Williams, January 22, 2018.

21. Pinheiro, *Violence Against Children*.

Running an orphanage in a developing country is a high-risk occupation. Quite apart from the obvious health, safety, and well-being issues, there are the financial pressures of keeping an institution open. The children need food and clothing. Paid staff need wages. If you rely on local networks and a relationship with foreign donors the situation becomes even more volatile. What happens if the donations dry up? What happens when relationships break down? There have been incidences of couples running orphanages and dividing the children between them when they get divorced. They then set up rival institutions![22]

Imagine the effect on the children. Imagine how dangerous and detrimental some of these places are, how detrimental to the welfare and development of the child. Imagine how much better things might be if these issues were approached in a professional, thoughtful, and systematic manner. Better still, imagine if family-based alternatives could be found. Wouldn't that be better for all concerned, for care providers, communities, and societies, and, most importantly, better for the child?

Myanmar, 2010. David and I address groups of orphanage directors and staff. At the close of each session, David poses them a question.

"If you or your wife died today, where would you want your children to be?"

He outlines four options: a large orphanage with around a hundred children; a medium-sized one of around fifty; a small, intimate family-unit-style institution; or, finally, a family home either with relatives or extended family or with someone unrelated who would love and care for them. Of course, all the directors agree that the fourth option is best.

Then the objections start. This will never work in Myanmar. It's too poor. It's not Westernized, it's a military dictatorship. Orphanages are too well established. People want to send their children there. Besides, the country is 80 percent Buddhist and that makes it impossible for such Western ideas as ours to ever catch on.

The objections keep coming. We address one, only for another to crop up. Of course, both David and I are aware of the real reasons for the objections. There is no shortage of well-meaning Christians only too willing to support orphanages. If Heaven's Family won't support them, they'll soon find another agency that will.

22. Cathleen Jones (founder of Children in Families), in discussion with Philip Williams, March 27, 2018.

It is a situation David knows only too well. Heaven's Family lost donors and supporters when it changed its emphasis.

> I have spent hundreds of hours in Christian and ostensibly Christian-run orphanages. There is no question in my mind that children are much better off in stable, cohesive, loving family units. If this is not possible with the child's biological family, then an extended family or foster family it's still much better—hands down—for children to be in families even if those families don't have the same level of Christian zeal as some of the orphanage directors.[23]

We were both naive at first when it came to convincing the orphanage directors. We knew it wasn't simple, that running an orphanage provided an income that might otherwise be hard to find. We weren't expecting them to suddenly close their institutions down. Nor would it be right for them to do so without alternatives in place. We had assumed, however, that all we had to do was present our watertight case and they would adopt a new perspective. We soon found out it wasn't as easy as that. As well as the financial incentives, there were significant cultural, social, and historical factors. Orphanages were simply part of the way things worked. There was little evidence of an alternative in a culture where Buddhist monasteries take in hundreds of children, all dressed like mini-monks. If the Buddhists did this to raise the next generation of monks, surely the Christians should do the same to train up the next generation of evangelists? The children were being fed, clothed, and educated; what possible objection could there be?

That first visit to Myanmar was hard work. David remembers me presenting our case gently and rationally, without making value judgments, without finding fault.[24] I must have cloaked my irritation and frustration. It felt like knocking at a stone wall. Inwardly, I was fuming. I kept wanting to say, "Look! Don't you understand? This is what a child needs!" I kept hearing what I've heard over so many years in so many countries around the world. "Our orphanage isn't like that. Ours is different." They might well be different, but we know that children want a family, need a family, deserve a family, and thrive far better in a safe and secure home. Unknown to me, my words did resonate with some of my listeners. I had not reckoned on Pastor Myint Nwye. I had not reckoned on my interpreter, Joney Hup.

---

23. D. Servant, discussion.
24. D. Servant, discussion.

When the package containing my notes, slides, and a transcript of my talks arrives in advance of my visit, Joney sets to work. His English is excellent, but he does find phrases that will not easily translate into Burmese. There is no equivalent term for "foster care" in any of the Burmese dialects he knows. He links several words and phrases together to find the closest match. He is intrigued by what he reads. As he translates for me, often in the teeth of objections, he becomes even more intrigued. He considers the implications. He runs an orphanage himself. Now he's translating for someone who challenges that concept.

Joney studied for a theological doctorate in the Philippines in 2007 and returned to Myanmar to set up a residential home in the time-honored fashion. It was a model he knew well but one he was to grow increasingly uncomfortable with. He remembers an occasion when a boy came to his orphanage from another institution nearby. The boy was unhappy there and wanted to stay with Joney instead. As Joney asked some questions, he discovered that the boy's parents were still alive so he offered to reunite him with them. The boy immediately protested. He did not want to go home.

"Why not? You could be back with your parents, with people who love you."

"No, they do not love me. I don't want to go home."

"How can you say that? They are your family. Of course they love you."

"They cannot possibly love me. Otherwise, they would not have sent me to the orphanage."[25]

For Joney, this was the turning point. The boy's family believed they were doing the right thing. The orphanage could surely do more for him then they could themselves. It was an act of love to send him there. The boy thought otherwise. No one had asked his opinion. He felt abandoned, rejected, alone.

Joney still runs a residential home, but it now acts as a transitional base as he works to integrate children into families. He travels into the hills and talks to the villagers and elders. He explains how it is better for their children to remain at home, not to be sent to institutions. People listen and understand.

In Yangon, Pastor Myint Nwye understood it already. He just hadn't heard anyone else articulate what he already knew. He came to hear me speak, with a sparkle in his eye and wearing his *longyi*, a sarong-like traditional skirt worn by both Burmese men and women. After I had spoken, he

---

25. Joney Hup, in discussion with Philip Williams, March 22, 2018.

came and thanked me. He understands English and can speak it reasonably well. He was not connected with Heaven's Family in any way. He was working independently. He told me I'd confirmed everything he already knew and given him what he needed to carry on. He was reuniting children from orphanages with their birth families where possible and finding other care providers if not. People criticized him, told him what he was doing was a disgrace. His fellow orphanage directors even accused him of not being Burmese! Yet he persisted. He knew it was right. When I asked him how he knew that, he smiled sadly.

"My parents sent me to an orphanage for education," he said. "I was unhappy there. I was scared, lonely, and missed my family. I cried many times until, eventually, my parents took me back home. That's how I know children don't belong in orphanages."

We are in the hill country. As I address a group of orphanage directors and close my presentation, Joney Hup is aware of my discomfort. He can tell I am struggling to answer some objections, he knows I understand little as yet of the conditions in his country. Yet something sparks within him as he translates my final, desperate remarks.

"Why not in Myanmar? If it is possible in Cambodia and Thailand and many other countries, why not Myanmar?"

My frustration boils over into a declaration that motivates him from that moment on.

"Look, even if you do not believe it now, it will happen. It is going to happen. It will happen here in Myanmar."[26]

---

26. Hup, discussion.

8. Children, Not Labels

IT STOLE AWAY OUR INDIVIDUALITY AND DIGNITY.
—STEPHEN UCEMBE[1]

LET'S CALL HIM FRED. He's an affable American backpacker who's just turned up at a Brazilian children's home offering to help. It's 1997 and Brenda and I are part way through our time at the mission station. Fred is enthusiastic, keen to work with kids. Surely another volunteer would be welcome? When I hear Fred's on-site I approach the directors. Have they checked him out?

"It's all above board, Mick. He's brought a reference from his pastor. It's alright for him to work with children."

"And you took his word for it? Did you check the reference?"

"Why shouldn't we believe him?"

"I remind them that Brenda and I were police-checked before we left the UK, that we were interviewed by the missionary organization before we were accepted. They checked our documents. Are they now prepared to accept a reference they haven't confirmed?"

"Ah—what do you suggest we do?"

"Check him out. Ring the guy's pastor to see if it's legit."

"I'll tell you what," one of the leaders says. "Why don't you have lunch with the guy, see what you make of him."

Over lunch Fred tells me that he travels regularly around Latin America. He will stay two or three months then return to the US to earn some money to fund his next trip. I report back to the directors.

1. Ucembe, "My Experience," lines 34–35.

"I can't say whether he's safe or not. I don't trust him and would never leave him with my own children. If we wouldn't trust someone with our own children, why should we trust them with someone else's? I've got an idea. Let's suggest that rather than working directly with the children he can help by tending the vegetable patch?"

The directors like this suggestion. They ask Fred if he would mind working with the horticultural team. The next day he's gone. We wake up in the morning and he's disappeared.

Matheus was dead. We heard the news as we renewed our visas over Christmas 1997. Brenda and I were stunned. We were fond of little Matheus and his sister. He loved to be talked to, taken to the play area. He would totter along despite his illness, all smiles. We were gutted. Worse, if this news weren't already bad enough, we learned that his death was entirely avoidable. Someone had taken over a shift and not been reminded about his medication. Matheus died, with the medication that would have saved his life within easy reach. He died from a breakdown in communication, from a lack of professional systems. He died from well-meaning amateurism.

I share these two stories to make a vital point. When it comes to childcare in voluntary settings, common sense regularly flies out of the window. When we first applied to go to Brazil I was shocked at how the various mission and development agencies saw no need for a qualified social worker. I then saw firsthand how the absence of professional input could have serious consequences. It is a pattern I have seen repeated time and again around the world. It isn't that professionals don't make mistakes. All over the world there have been high-profile cases where professional foster care programs have gone badly wrong. A key principle Isa Guará and her colleagues insisted upon when I first met them was how Brazilian social workers could learn from our mistakes so as not to repeat them.[2]

Care plans and case recording are a critical part of SFAC's training programs. It's about meticulous planning, accurate records: who, what, how, where, when. So often we find a lack of proper documentation and procedures in residential childcare institutions. A written record is essential so that people don't rely on memory. How often in our own families, even with just two or three children, do we forget or overlook things? "I thought you had told him!" "You knew it was my mother's birthday; we always go around then!" How much more important then, is it to have written records

2. Statement from Isa Guará, trans. Delton Hochstedler, April 26, 2018.

and procedures so that paid staff and volunteers know what to do for each child? Individual care is so often lacking where institutions allow details of a child's particular needs to get lost. As in the case of Matheus, mistakes can be fatal.

The best-intentioned programs can fail unless we apply a rigorous and professional approach. It hardly needs to be said that schemes and institutions that rely heavily on volunteers or short-term staff are laying themselves wide open to problems with continuity, attention to detail, and lack of systems. If it's true that there is an orphanage industry, it's also true that there is a short-term aid and development and mission industry. It has become part of what's become known as voluntourism.[3] It is done with the best of intentions. Churches, universities, youth organizations, all encourage young people to spend time abroad helping with development projects. In the case of students, it can impress a potential employer. It provides evidence of practical work and enterprise overseas. It demonstrates you are a caring and compassionate person. It all sounds so wonderful, so convincing. A group of students digging a well, kicking a football around, painting a mural. Then they all jump back into the minibus, return to the airport and fly away forever. Imagine the impact this has on children who already feel abandoned and alone? How would you feel if you were lonely and confused and a bunch of lively, friendly strangers suddenly arrive? They play with you, cuddle you, and organize exciting games and crafts. Then, as suddenly as they came, they disappear. What has happened to your newly found friends? You feel bereft, more abandoned than you did before. Within a few days or weeks, another minibus pulls up. More young and lively strangers arrive. The pattern begins all over again.

Let's be clear. I am not suggesting that it is wrong to visit a community project or even a school, but in a residential childcare setting, the consequences can be devastating. The problems are compounded when visitors expect to interact with the children, even if their visit is in connection with something else. Even very recently I saw a mission website promote the opportunity to hold and hug a baby as a prime incentive for joining a short-term program! Visitors assume that when a child approaches them for a hug or to hold their hand they are doing it to show affection. Trained social workers and child psychologists recognize that when an institutionalized child pays attention to an adult it indicates a deep sense of loss, a lack of attachment. That is why the child wants to hug you or hold your hand.

---

3. For voluntourism as it applies to orphanages, see Riley, "Volunteers."

They crave the security of adult affirmation and protection. How cruel to offer the child a fleeting taste of this only for it to be quickly and repeatedly removed? Don't we all teach our children to be wary of strangers? Voluntourism contributes to a higher risk of physical and sexual abuse, especially with younger children. It can lead to emotional harm through repeated patterns of connection and loss. It creates insecurity and uncertainty through fleeting and multiple relationships. Not only that, what is its purpose? Who benefits? The volunteer? The host organization? Surely not the child.

There are, of course, plenty of very worthwhile community projects run by charities and NGOs where funding and voluntary support are deployed responsibly and effectively. Some models can be misunderstood, for all the best efforts charities make to explain the processes to their donors. Philip Aspegren has extensive experience of both institutional and family-based care. He knows how the various funding models work and is aware of the problems some can create for all involved—the supporters as well as the children they seek to help.

> One of the issues we have, particularly with the North American model of child sponsorship, is that it conveys a sense of *ownership*. The individual donors or sponsors are encouraged to think that they *own* that child, in the sense that it is their money that is paying for its support. They might donate, what, $25 a month? It may take five or six sponsors to support each child, perhaps $150–200 a month per child. Family-based alternative care doesn't quite work that way. It's a model that doesn't lend itself to that simple an approach.[4]

It can also raise ethical concerns. In many child sponsorship schemes the funds go to projects in the child's community rather than directly to their family. They are community support projects rather than individual sponsorship programs. It's great that the villages and townships benefit but donors can misunderstand how the system works, even though reputable charities explain it to them.[5] Child sponsorship can lead to children feeling left out or disadvantaged if they aren't the subjects of such programs. My colleagues and I have been asked by African children whether we were their sponsors. On one occasion, a coworker had to tell a small boy that he wasn't his new sponsor. The child said that he must be truly unlikeable.

4. Aspegren, discussion.

5. When World Vision attempted to rebrand its child sponsorship program as family sponsorship schemes, its donations dropped by half. See Joyce, *Child Catchers*, 237.

His brother had sponsors, but nobody was sponsoring him. How do you explain a situation like that to a child?

It's nearing Christmas and the phone rings in the office at Leeds City Council. It's another of the calls we get each Christmas, a well-meaning and well-heeled person on the line.

"Have you got a child who could come and spend Christmas with us? We'll give them the time of their lives. We'll give them a Christmas they will never forget!"

The child would never forget it alright, but for reasons other than these people expect. Imagine a one- or two-day blast of Christmas cheer and comfort, only for it to end as suddenly as it began? One day you are in a warm, comfortable home which exceeds your wildest dreams. The next, you are whisked away, back to your plain food, your basic living conditions, the lack of adult care and attention. How easy it is to do all the wrong things for all the right reasons! Or for our own benefit, our own glowing sense of self-fulfillment and achievement.

When it comes to residential institutions in tourist spots, there are even worse issues to contend with. Voluntourism fuels the institutionalization and even trafficking of children. It costs money to run a residential institution. You have to feed and clothe the children, pay workers, fund repairs to buildings and equipment. When you are relying on donations from wealthy Westerners, why not invite them in to see the children? They can play with the kids and take selfies to post on social media. It is all part of the experience of international travel, all part of the tour. An orphanage director needs all the funds he or she can obtain. If wealthy Western visitors want to come and play with the children and pay for the privilege, why ignore that opportunity? Yes, it means the orphanage has to be clean and presentable and the children well clothed and fed, otherwise, the visitors will stop coming. But to attract them in the first place requires one essential ingredient; cute and appealing children. Where are they found? If they aren't real orphans or street children, there is only one place they can come from. Their families. In the most extreme cases, recruiters pay families to abandon their children or else persuade them with slick and persuasive presentations. It is a form of modern slavery. At last, it is an issue that governments and legislators are seeking to address.

On April 18, 2018, I attended a briefing in the British Parliament led by Senator Linda Reynolds from Australia.[6] British MPs and representatives of charities and NGOs learned about recent measures the Australian government is taking to tackle the issue. The Australian Parliament is the first legislature to identify "orphanage trafficking" as a category of modern slavery. In 2017 Australia's Joint Standing Committee on Foreign Affairs, Defence and Trade defined it as, "the active recruitment of children from families and communities into residential care institutions . . . for the purpose of foreign funding and voluntourism."[7] Anti-modern slavery and trafficking legislation is going through the Australian Parliament at the time of writing.

Cathleen Jones, of Children in Families in Cambodia, has seen the problems associated with voluntourism and orphanage tourism firsthand.[8] When Cathleen and her husband Dale ran an orphanage, people often offered to come and paint a mural or play with the children. She told them that this wasn't what was required but she would happily accommodate them if they could teach English or another skill. Their enthusiasm immediately dropped. Some even withdrew their financial support. The key issue, though, is that this kind of well-intentioned but often ill-considered activity can and does cause real harm.

Kathryn Joyce puts it like this: "Voluntourism frequently amounts to a deprofessionalization of missionary work, a shift from career missionaries who learn the language, culture, and laws of the country to amateurs combining sightseeing and charity."[9] Craig Greenfield, another care reform practitioner, writing about his experiences in Cambodia, describes how

---

6. "Modern Slavery, Orphanage Trafficking, Deinstitutionalisation and the Faith Sector," a special meeting with Senator Linda Reynolds, April 18, 2018, Portcullis House, Westminster. I was invited by Home for Good, a UK charity that shares SFAC's ethos of finding a family home as the gold standard for global childcare.

7. Australia Government, *Hidden in Plain Sight*. For one Christian group's guidance on what such legislation means for the local church in Australia, see ACCI Missions & Relief, *Short-Term Missions*.

8. Jones, discussion.

9. Joyce, *Child Catchers*, 7. Joyce cites a 2010 report from southern Africa which contends that all too often, "the emotional needs of the tourists are the key focus of these trips, as visitors seek personal fulfilment by forging immediate emotional connections with orphanage children. But after the tourists leave, the children suffer yet another abandonment, leading to a pattern of intense connection and loss that is detrimental to their emotional well-being and development."

short-term volunteers can inadvertently create dependency and under-mine grassroots community initiatives.[10]

> If there was one thing I had learned in the slums of Phnom Penh, it was the classic dictum, "Never do for someone what they can do for themselves." I saw Westerners, particularly short-term teams, repeatedly ignoring this principle as they arrived in town for two weeks to build and paint churches and schools, taking away from poor Cambodians the one thing they have to contribute, the sweat of their brow. Denying them the dignity of helping themselves.[11]

I would add an additional observation. It can also prevent them from getting paid. Do we want to help people to support their families? If so, then let's start paying them a decent wage!

Yes, there are ways that short-term teams can augment long-term projects. Many mission agencies and secular aid and relief projects recognize that and deploy volunteers accordingly. They don't replace work that can be done by local people or long-term workers; they work alongside them and complement what they do.[12] I experienced this at the Brazilian mission station. For what felt like an eternity, I painted the equipment in the play area, replaced old or dangerous planks, and repaired components. I could have felt a little miffed. Here was I, a qualified social worker, doing repair work. In this instance, the contribution was important to the project. You only had to see the smiles on the children's faces and their joy and delight when playing on the refurbished equipment to appreciate its long-term value. Besides, I carried out the work alongside other duties that did draw on my professional background.

If my comments on voluntourism sound unnecessarily harsh, most of us involved with SFAC have done exactly this sort of thing ourselves. We speak from experience. We are childcare and child protection professionals, yet we too have made similar mistakes. We stress this point when we speak to individuals and organizations around the world. We are not pointing the finger. We are not beating ourselves up nor are we beating anyone else up. We set out what we believe to be a far better approach and offer the training and support required to bring that about.

10. Greenfield, *Urban Halo*, 74.

11. Ibid.

12. Additional insights on this issue from Steve Bartel (YWAM/Formando Vidas), in discussion with Philip Williams, May 23, 2018. For more on Formando Vidas, see http://colombiastreetkids.org/.

The issues of voluntourism and orphanage tourism goes beyond minor irritations or wasted opportunities for local communities. It is part of a multimillion—some would say, multibillion—dollar industry. It creates a market. It creates demand. It creates the pull factors that draws tourists to visit institutions and the funds required to run them. It stimulates the push factors which drive the recruiters into the villages and onto the streets looking for children to fill their institutions. It creates a vicious circle. It is a circle we must break out of if we are to see any lasting change.

The response of the Australian government is a very welcome development. All our work through SFAC is based on solid research into children's needs and a concern for children's rights. Everything we say, every issue we provide training on, is in tune with international conventions on the rights of the child. Whether it's our position on professionalism, on strengthening families, on religion and culture; it's all based on agreed international standards and directed toward the best interests of the child. There is a growing momentum across governments and NGOs to find family-based alternatives to traditional institutional childcare. The United Nations Convention on the Rights of the Child (UNCRC) came into force in September 1990. All United Nations member countries have ratified the UNCRC apart from the United States. Although the US government was actively involved in drafting the UNCRC and signed it in February 1995, no US president has so far submitted it to the Senate for consultation and ratification.[13]

Article 20 of the UNCRC stipulates that where children are temporarily or permanently unable to remain with their family, the state has a responsibility to provide "special protection and assistance."[14] This should be in accordance with their national laws and should respect ethnic, religious, cultural, and linguistic background. As SFAC seeks to understand cultural and contextual conditions, we almost invariably find principles we all share in common. In Islamic societies care of vulnerable children is seen as a "communal obligation." The Muslim model of kinship care, *kafaalah*, is recognized both by the UNCRC and by the United Nations Guidelines for the Alternative Care of Children.[15] A key principle is the preservation of the

---

13. For a full list of signatories, see https://treaties.un.org/pages/viewdetails.aspx?src=treaty&mtdsg_no=iv-11&chapter=4&lang=en.

14. UNCRC, art. 20.1.

15. Article 20 of the UNCRC states: "State Parties shall in accordance with their national laws ensure alternative care for such a child. Such care could include, inter alia, foster placement, *kafaalah* of Islamic law, adoption or if necessary placement in suitable institutions for the care of children." Paragraph 2(b) of the Guidelines have: "To support

child's biological heritage. It is essential that the bloodline is respected and acknowledged. It is an established social work practice to provide a "life story book" with details of the child's lineage to enable adoptive or foster families to inform them of their origins and identity. It is an instance where professional good practice dovetails with religious and cultural beliefs.[16] The UNCRC cites foster care or kinship care options and adoption as possible measures and, "if necessary placement in suitable institutions for the care of children."[17] The clear implication is that institutional care should only be considered if alternatives are not available. In other words, they should be the final and not the first and only port of call. Again, we see the core principles defined and applied. The key in each and every instance should be the best interests of the child.

If we want to know what children really want and really need, we should ask them.

Children and young people living with foster families took part in an independent review of foster care in England published in February 2018. The findings were not at all surprising.

> When asked what children most want from their foster family, the overwhelming majority indicated that they wanted to feel like part of the family. Many young people also suggested that they would like increased financial support. For teenagers this tended to be support for day-to-day activities, whereas young children expressed that they would like subsidised access to extracurricular activities. Young people of all ages expressed that they would like a greater role in the decision making process.[18]

A sense of belonging, access to sources of funding and support, more say in what happens to them. These are what these English children living in local government care wanted most. Why should it be any different in other parts of the world? Does anyone ever ask the children in an unregistered orphanage in Indonesia or Uganda what they want? Does anyone ask them how it feels to be separated from their family and very often their culture? To have to sing, dance, and perform on cue for Western visitors and tourists? If Cathleen

---

efforts to keep children in, or return them to, the care of their family or, failing this, to find another appropriate and permanent solution, including adoption and *kafaalah* of Islamic law."

16. For more on Islamic approaches, see Karim, *Adoption and Fostering*.

17. UNCRC, art. 20.3.

18. Narey and Owers, *Foster Care*, 121.

Jones and other former orphanage directors are disturbed by the effects of voluntourism, how must it feel to experience it as an "orphan"? Stephen Ucembe has. He grew up in a Kenyan orphanage. He now works for the NGO Hope and Homes for Children. He describes how it feels to be "gawked" at by visitors, treated like a zoo animal. He remembers how they were paraded without shoes to gain more sympathy and attract more donations.

> The institution staff had taught us a routine . . . . as soon as the visitors arrived in tour vans we had to exude joy. Indeed, we jumped up and down, and raptured in unison with song and dance that welcomed them.
>
> We knew that the only way to ensure they came back again to help the institution was by how much they smiled at our entertainment, and by the tears, sadness or sympathy that came when they were told that we were "orphans". I remember the senior staff on duty . . . pronouncing how some of us had been abandoned by their parents, how others had been picked from the streets and others rejected by families. The majority of us often dropped our heads in shame and embarrassment during these introductions. The term orphan, although sometimes used with good intentions, had become a homogenizing and pathologizing label. It stole away our individuality and dignity.[19]

Narel and Alison Atkinson run the Home of Hope, a temporary residential care center in Colombo, Sri Lanka, where children are supported until such time as they can be reunited with their families. Their work in the slums is all about providing the support and resources local people need to care for their own. The Atkinsons established a traditional orphanage in the wake of the 2004 Indian Ocean tsunami but gradually came to appreciate the value of family-based alternatives. They know how important it is to ask the right questions, to start from the child's perspective. As with so many of us, it was a lesson they learned the hard way. Ranga was a street boy whose mother had fallen on hard times. The family was homeless and he was being drawn into the shady world of drug dealers and pimps. The Atkinsons took him, his younger siblings and other relatives into their children's home. Eventually, they helped Ranga's mother find basic accommodation. She started work and conditions improved. When Ranga left the home, reunited with his mother, he turned to Narel and delivered a furious tirade.

"If you hadn't taken me from my mother, I could have stayed with her all this time."

19. Ucembe, "My Experience," lines 19–35.

Narel was devastated. They had done everything they could to help this child and now he hated them for it. No one asked Ranga what he'd wanted. They had simply assumed what they were doing was right. The Atkinsons resolved to seek professional assistance to better understand the issues in a more holistic and integrated way.[20] Ranga's reaction is common. What he wanted most had been taken away from him. Such incidents illustrate the importance of "gatekeeping." This is the process that ensures that alternative care for children is used only when necessary and that the child receives the most appropriate support for their individual needs. It requires careful assessment and clearly defined thresholds to determine which children require alternative care and which can remain with their families with suitable support. It is another example of professional practice and one where SFAC can provide assistance, advice, and training.[21]

Children are children, not labels. If we are going to use labels, then surely, child is the best one? They are human beings, not exhibits or tourist attractions. As a label orphan can be inaccurate and misleading. It is a loaded term. It conjures up images of a lonely, abandoned, and needy child. If we treat children as children we begin to consider what they really need, not what we assume from the label. It is clear that many so-called orphans have one or more parents still alive. UNICEF estimated in 2017 that of 140 million children classed as orphans worldwide, only some 15.1 million have lost both parents.[22] Fifteen million sounds like a problem, 140 million like a crisis. By far the vast majority of children labelled as orphans live with a surviving parent, grandparent, or other family member. Some believe that misunderstandings and misapplication of the term "orphan" led to the apparent "orphan crisis," the growth of unregistered children's homes and the orphanage tourism that governments and NGOs are seeking to redress.[23] We all know that every child, regardless of labels, needs a safe, loving, stable, and secure family. They need somewhere to belong, somewhere they can thrive.

One of the myths surrounding institutional care is that it is cheaper and more efficient than the slow, painstaking process of finding family- and

20. A. Atkinson, discussion.

21. For more on gatekeeping, see Gale and Csáky, *Making Decisions* and Better Care Network, "Gatekeeping."

22. UNICEF, "Orphans," line 6.

23. For a hard-hitting presentation on these issues, see Cheney, "Orphan Industrial Complex."

community-based alternatives. The opposite is the case. Save the Children found residential care in central and eastern Africa to be ten times more expensive than family- or community-based alternatives. In the Kagera region of Tanzania, the World Bank found that the annual cost for a child in residential care was approximately six times higher than supporting a child in foster care.[24]

> The money that goes to sustain these institutions could instead be targeted at caring for much larger numbers of children within families. The bottom line is that programs to keep children within their own communities, surrounded by neighbors, friends and families that they know and love are ultimately much cheaper— both financially and in terms of emotional cost to the child.[25]

It makes sense financially. It makes sense psychologically. It makes sense for the individual child. If the will is there and the resources and support can be found, then surely, it's a no-brainer?

What's stopping us from doing it? What's preventing it from happening? The reasons are complex and varied. There are vested interests and money to be made. Mark Riley is a fiery and passionate Welshman who is now a technical advisor for Hope and Homes for Children and Maestral. He has lived and worked in Uganda for some years reuniting children with their families. He has had punches thrown at him by adoption agency workers and missionaries. He's received legal threats and been intimidated online.[26] People often oppose change. It may threaten the status quo, their livelihood, or contradict what they believe is right. The opposition may come from ignorance, naivety, or a lack of professional insight. Even the best-intentioned individuals and organizations can fail to grasp the potential harm caused to vulnerable children by residential care. Once people understand the issues for themselves we can all work together for lasting change. We can all work in the best interests of the child.

24. For the relative costs of alternative care, see Doyle, *Misguided Kindness*, 7; Williamson and Greenberg, *Families, Not Orphanages*, 7. Both cite estimates that residential care in South Africa can cost up to four times more than foster care and six times more than providing care for children within their own families.

25. Doyle, *Misguided Kindness*, 7.

26. Mark Riley, in discussion with Philip Williams, April 19, 2018.

Mam and Dad with Pam

The only photo of Pam I saw as a child.

Pam and I on our last family holiday
before she was sent away.

Uganda: where the child-headed household lived. It has now been rebuilt.

Uganda: the eldest boy prepares supper.

Ongoing support: Dan Hope with a Ugandan boy at a school run by CALM Africa.

Cambodia: Me with foster families.

Myanmar: Water reaches a Chin village.

India: Caitlin Lance Hope leads a training exercise.

Brazil: A certificate and two smiles. I'm not showing my teeth!

Brazil: Dr. Deni and I sign a declaration to prioritize family-based care.

Brazil: Job's a good 'un. More smiles as a conference closes.

At home with our family.

Mick and Brenda Pease.

9. The Breakthrough Begins

OKAY, LET ME ASK YOU ALL A QUESTION.

It's hot and sticky. There's no electricity. I am scribbling notes and headings on a blackboard for my Chin interpreter to transmit to forty orphanage directors. We have been training there for several days, sat on benches or on the floor of a windowless chapel. It is called Ebenezer like so many in industrial Yorkshire, yet we are in the Burmese hills close to the Indian border. The chapel is part of an orphanage complex that looks like a prison camp. It was built immediately after the Second World War and paid for by Japanese reparations. David Servant has summoned the orphanage directors Heaven's Family supports in that region to come and hear me speak. He takes a hard line. If they don't come and hear me, he will no longer provide ongoing support. We had tried reason on my first visit. This time, David's more drastic.

I have no computer, no PowerPoint slides, only my notes, a blackboard, and a piece of chalk. I describe foster care, kinship care, and alternatives to residential childcare. I explain what it looks like and why it's becoming the preferred model of childcare in numerous developing countries. As I'm in mid-flow an elderly lady rises to her feet. She is older than all the others and clearly held in some respect. I later find that she comes from an even more remote area, from Hakha, capital of Chin State, some 6,120 feet above sea level. She challenges me in broken English.

"The trouble with people like you," she says accusingly. "Is that you come here and think your Western principles will work in our Asian context. You don't understand the Asian ways and culture and what you are talking about are Western ideas."

I'm taken aback. I did not expect this. I ask the interpreter to convey her words to the other orphanage directors to give me time to think. I see them nod in agreement. They begin to mutter among themselves. I am completely flummoxed. I cannot fall back on my slides. I don't have my charts and statistics. I do have a piece of chalk and an interpreter. I think and quickly pray, "Lord, you've got to help me here! I'm right on the spot!"

After a moment or two, I say, "Okay, let me ask you all a question. How many of you are looking after children you are related to in some way?"

The interpreter presents the question and they begin to murmur again. They start to raise their hands one by one. Soon, every single one has raised their hand. They all look after children they are related to biologically but who are not their own.

"Congratulations!" I say. "You are already looking after the children of relatives. Kinship care in Myanmar is alive and well. Well done! Now here is a tricky one—and I know you are all directors of orphanages, but how many of you are caring for children in your own family that you are not related to?"

Again, the mutter and hum. Again, every hand rises.

"Congratulations!" I say again. "What is that if it is not foster care? It is a concept you are already familiar with. It's not an alien concept at all. You are already doing it if you are looking after someone else's child in your own home. It is not a Westernized principle, it is a global principle. It is a human response to children in need. You are already doing it informally. What I am talking about it is doing it in a formalized way."

They begin to nod. The buzz continues and rises.

The elderly female orphanage director was silent from that point onward. I visited Hakha on a later visit. I saw her orphanage and it was a shocker. David Servant and his team were also horrified. They had supported this orphanage with sponsorship from Western donors for many years but were unable to visit due to restrictions imposed by the military regime. Once they saw it they immediately began to withdraw their support. Instead of using the donations to improve the quality of care, the old woman had simply built extra dormitories to accommodate even more children. The bitter irony, of course, was that the approach she championed as an indigenous Burmese solution was itself a Western import. It was a system imported in colonial times, one that the West itself had long abandoned.

Hakha became a strategic landmark for Heaven's Family as it changed direction and emphasis. It was the first place where Philip Barker, a former

British Army soldier and mechanical engineer, weaned an orphanage away from reliance on international support. It raised its own funds and became self-sufficient. That was a first step and an important one. The plan at that time was to encourage the orphanages to raise their own funds by small business enterprises. By now, the children were cared for in smaller, family-sized groups with a view to eventual reintegration into their community. In the first instance, an attempt would be made to return the child to their biological family, with measures in place to provide practical support. If this proved unfeasible for whatever reason (drug or alcohol abuse, incapacity of some kind), then the child's wider family, uncles, aunts, grandparents could become involved. If no blood relatives were available then, against all the odds, they would look for foster families.

I cannot overestimate the scale and complexity of the transition Heaven's Family made. David and his team directed donations to orphanages in nine countries. Now their work with children and families is focused on three.[1] They lost some supporters but gained others. They also helped individuals and organizations they were already working with to see things from their new perspective.

> I am not proud of the work we did before we met Mick. Yes, we had done some good things, we had taken kids off the streets, clothed them, fed them, given them a roof over their heads, an education. All that was great, but what we hadn't done was to realize that there was so much more, that vital sense of attachment, of belonging. We acted in good faith. We were not aware of other models at that time.[2]

Philip Barker now coordinates a team of six social workers in Yangon seeking to reunite children with their biological families, supporting parents and wider kinship groups, finding substitute families where possible or where necessary. As video case studies demonstrate, foster care is gaining traction.[3]

> It feels like a drop in the ocean, at times. When I tell people what we are doing they say, "That sounds like a hiding to nothing, that's going to take years!" Then I think of the encouragement Mick's given us, and that's quite something coming from someone with as

1. Philip Barker, in discussion with Philip Williams, January 29, 2018; Stephen Servant, in discussion with Philip Williams, April 9, 2018.

2. D. Servant, discussion.

3. For example, see ACCI Missions & Relief, "Kinnected Myanmar."

much experience as he has. It's beginning to happen here in Myanmar because of that and because we've stayed to see it through.[4]

It is hot, sticky, and wet. We are higher up and the air is clearer except when the clouds descend upon the hills. There are steaming patches of jungle but most of the hills are shorn and bare from slash-and-burn agriculture. Villages cluster on the hilltops, a jumble of shacks and huts. The children run away when we approach. Their parents and older siblings pore over our faces and hands. They feel our skin. Most of these people have not seen white people for fifty years. An old man remembers the last foreigner they saw in these remote hills.

"British or American?" we ask. David and I have a jokey transatlantic rivalry running between us.

"British," the interpreters tell us. "The old man remembers the date. 1954. It was a missionary, and you are the first European he has seen since then."

"The British are back!" I tease David. "We were the last here and we're the first to return!"

Every November, David visited Myanmar to meet relief and development workers, missionaries, and orphanage directors. Travel was difficult and restricted. The military government prohibited outsiders from entering certain areas, particularly the northwestern hill country of the Chin people. David was keen to get up there. He wanted us to see what he calls the "source villages"—poor, Christianized Chin communities which provide most of the children for the orphanages. Christianity arrived in the region in the 1890s, brought by American missionaries. They found the tribal, animist hill peoples more open to their message than the Buddhist majority in the cities and the lowlands. Soon almost all churches and denominations sent missionaries to the region. Gradually a whole infrastructure developed of churches, seminaries, Bible schools, and orphanages.

As with other mission agencies I've worked with around the world, David and his team were surprised when they found that most of the children in the orphanages they supported were not actually orphans. One or more of their parents were often still alive. Yes, some of the children were abandoned. Others had parents incapacitated through drug abuse, mental health or similar issues. The vast majority were in these institutions because their parents had sent them there. They were there because they were poor.

4. Barker, discussion.

David and I soon realized that it was unrealistic to rely on all the orphanage directors to change their ways of working. After all, the orphanages were their livelihood. Instead, David and his team decided to consolidate their efforts around orphanage directors like Joney Hup and his vision for family-based care in Myanmar. The intention was to address the issues that led to children leaving the "source villages" for orphanages in the first place—poverty, lack of education opportunities at high-school level, and so on.[5] If Heaven's Family could direct resources to tackle these issues, perhaps they could begin to change hearts and minds. To do that we had first to assess the needs, visit the Chin villages, and find out what we could do.

Early one morning we set off from our hotel for a four-hour trip up into the hills. We piled into an ancient, military-style minibus, with a few guides and helpers alongside on motorbikes. We climbed upward on dirt tracks and jeep tracks. As we neared our destination, I saw something extraordinary. A concrete receptacle, a tank embedded into the hillside, fed water up to the village above by means of a narrow pipe. Our guides told us that this was the main water supply, fed by an ancient spring that had never been known to run dry. The water source must have been no more than two inches across, but it was constant. The water bubbled into the reservoir tank, paid for by Heaven's Family, and was conveyed upward by thin plastic pipes, completely by gravity. There were no hydraulics, no pumps. I know all about hydraulic machinery. I repaired complex moving parts underground at the coalface at Kellingley Colliery. This was an engineering feat such as I had never seen. Our guides explained it was all to do with the angle and diameter of the pipes. Astonished, I asked who was responsible.

"The villagers, with assistance from a local engineer."

By what looked to me like little short of a technical miracle the villagers had set the pipe in such a way that the water flowed up an incline for over half a mile and into the village to a purpose-built reservoir cistern. Every twenty yards or so they had set up a faucet stop and the village had constant access to clean, fresh water. They no longer sent their children half a mile down a steep hill with an empty bucket several times a day. Their ingenuity and resilience amazed and humbled me.

The example of the water pipe struck me as an object lesson. If these people could be this resourceful and innovative in providing water to the village, what else could they be capable of? Surely, they could apply such learning and resourcefulness to other projects that could benefit their

5. S. Servant, discussion.

community? With the right support and infrastructure, there was no reason why they could not foster abandoned or orphaned children. The support structures were already potentially in place. With some training and support, they could care for the children themselves.

As we visited the village, talking to the people, their elders and leaders, a motorcyclist pulled up with a message. The military wanted us to leave. The village elders asked us to sit down first. We were not to go anywhere until they had fed us and shown us hospitality. We could not dishonor them by leaving beforehand. They led out a pig, we heard its squeals, and before we left, we ate boiled pork and rice as protocol required.

Cambodia, 2006. It's high summer and I'm even hotter than I was in Myanmar. I address a group of foster parents, potential foster parents, and villagers. I'm told to "keep them entertained with an impromptu talk about foster care." It's completely unplanned. I do my best. I have no notes, no prepared speech. So, I talk. I talk about my own experiences, my observations, the things I have seen and learned. It gets hotter. I loosen the buttons on my shirt. It gets hotter still. I open my shirt and find my T-shirt underneath clinging to my skin. I'm melting.

"Poor Mick," Cathleen Jones remembers. "He rolled up his shirtsleeves, loosened his collar, rolled up his pants. He was almost a puddle before he was through. In the end, one of the villagers took pity on him and rigged up a fan to a car battery. I don't think he'd have been able to finish speaking otherwise."[6]

If I struggled with the heat, poor Cathleen struggled with my Yorkshire accent. She wasn't the only one. On my first visit her husband Dale took over the translation because the Cambodian interpreters couldn't follow me at all. After several visits, he handed me back to the Khmer interpreters. I'd learned to slow down! With much mirth, we also discovered the truth of the old adage that the Americans and British are separated by the same language.[7] On one occasion, Cathleen asked me what color pants I'd be wearing. I reacted in horror. "No one's seeing m'pants!" Cathleen cries in an attempt to mimic my accent which sounds more Scottish than Yorkshire.

6. Jones, discussion.

7. Variations of this saying have been attributed both to Oscar Wilde and George Bernard Shaw.

To the British, "pants" almost always refers to men's briefs or underpants. What Americans call pants, we call "trousers."[8]

It's my second visit and the first time I've seen foster care working in Southeast Asia. By that time, we had seen small but encouraging beginnings in Latin America. We had lobbied, pushed, cajoled, spoken at conferences, given training sessions. Trudge, trudge, trudge. Even after all that time I was still naive. I imagined it would happen first in an urban context, where the support systems were, the health care, the professional services. In Latin America the breakthrough came from small family-unit-sized orphanages on the outskirts of the cities where the children lived. Here in Cambodia and Southeast Asia the breakthrough came in the villages.

SFAC supported the work of Dale and Cathleen Jones for some years. They were former orphanage directors. They relied on donors and sponsors from the US, Australasia, and other Western countries. Now they too were working to reunite children with their families or to get them into kinship care or foster homes. Dale and Cathleen were already on this trajectory when I first met them at a conference organized by Chab Dai, a coalition of Christian agencies dedicated to combating sexual abuse, human trafficking, and exploitation, led at that time by Helen Sworn.[9]

Cathleen remembers that we provided theoretical and professional confirmation of the need to move away from institutional/residential solutions to family-based care.[10] I was invited to help inspire and train their team, provide practical insights, and evaluate their work. We struck up an immediate rapport. I was impressed by what I saw. Sometime later, SFAC was in a position to help fund some of their social work staff for a few years. Even so, on my second visit, I remained skeptical of the possibility of foster care gaining ground in rural Cambodia. I was even more skeptical when Cathleen told me about the three children she had eventually persuaded the authorities to release to take part in a pilot project. Sam Ang was around three years old, institutionalized and completely blind. There were also two girls, both about two years old, one with cystic fibrosis requiring around-the-clock attention. The other was blind in one eye. If someone was out to test our mettle, they could not have come up with children with more

8. Jones, discussion.

9. Chab Dai means "joining hands" in Khmer. The network was established in 2005 by British missionary and activist Helen Sworn. See http://chabdai.org/. See also Marshall, "Need Plus Greed."

10. Jones, discussion.

challenging needs. I had seen the conditions in Cambodian villages. These children would struggle in the most advanced environments, with access to the latest technology and specialist care. How were they going to cope in a very basic Cambodian village, some twenty minutes by motorcycle along mud tracks from the nearest main road?

I had reckoned without Annee. I had reckoned without the very evident love and care I saw among the Cambodian foster families that day. Cathleen saw my face light up as I saw how it worked.[11] Annee was a key worker within Children in Families, a tireless advocate for family-based care. This was her home village and she had been there month after month, talking to the people, explaining the concept, evaluating their capacity to foster and to care. Several families volunteered. They liked what they had heard. They wanted to give it a try.

Houses in rural Cambodia are pretty sparse, essentially a platform of bamboo and wooden props, all strapped together, with gaps to allow air to circulate. Roofs are thatched or made from tin or tarpaulin. Families eat, sleep, and cook in the same space. Cathleen laughs as she recalls a comment by a well-meaning Western supporter. Were they going to provide plastic mattress coverings for those children who might continue to wet their beds? Cathleen explained that they don't have beds. They sleep on mats on platforms raised on stilts above the rats and cockroaches, the ants, insects, and snakes.[12]

Sam Ang's foster parents already had two children. I visited them in their tiny home and couldn't imagine how the four of them could survive in such limited space, let alone a blind boy. His foster father was a "bike boy." He earned his meager living conveying people to town on the back of his motorbike. They had little money and few possessions. Did they know what they were taking on?

I was full of questions for Annee, Dale, and Cathleen. How are you assessing these families? What kind of background checks are you carrying out? The families might be safe and secure, but what about the rest of the villagers? How did they know that the kids wouldn't wander off? That people wouldn't attack or molest them? Gradually, it dawned on me. Annee knew these people. Everyone knew everyone else. They were the eyes and ears of the community. With some basic training and support, these people

11. Ibid.
12. Ibid.

were perfectly capable of looking after these children. I could see it with my own eyes.

There is a video on the Children in Families website which shows Sam Ang and his foster family.[13] He is supremely happy, well-adjusted, and loved; a completely different child to the one who spent his first two years in a stark orphanage. Like so many younger children in institutions, he rocked back and forth, banged his head, self-harmed. Now, he was loved by his foster family and across the wider community. When I returned about two or three years later, I was intrigued to find that they had laid a sandy path so that Sam Ang could find his way around. He knew he was walking in the right direction when he felt sand rather than grass beneath his feet. When I asked the villagers whose remarkably effective idea this was, they told me that they had thought of it themselves. Nobody from outside told them what to do. Their own ingenuity and resourcefulness provided the solution. The two girls thrived too, although sadly the one with cystic fibrosis died in 2017. She spent her short life in a caring family home, not confined to a cot in an institution.

Here, out in the villages, there was care and concern, there was love. It all made so much sense now. In the rural areas, overheads were low, the cost of living less than in the busy, bustling towns. In the cities, people were paying high rents and holding down several jobs to make ends meet. They had no capacity to take on additional children. Although life was harder in rural areas the social networks were in place. People had time to devote to the children. They had the ingenuity and the resilience. They could make it work.

Children in Families took the principles I'd shared and applied them beyond my expectations. It was also in Cambodia that I sensed that something was in the air. It was a like a breeze blowing through the stickiness and humidity. For a decade I had felt like a lone voice. Now I was hearing other people saying the same thing, saying it loudly, saying it strong. Cathleen suggested I meet a good friend of hers, someone as passionate as I was about getting abandoned children into families. She was Australian, well-informed, dynamic, and very direct. I thought we were forthright in Yorkshire, but from what I'd heard, she took no prisoners. Her name was Rebecca Nhep.

13. See Foley, "From Lonely Orphan to Loved Son."

10. Love to Share

I HAVE ENOUGH LOVE FOR MORE.

—PATRICIA, A UGANDAN FOSTER MOTHER[1]

REBECCA NHEP BENT MY ear, and quite literally, my neck, during a three-hour drive to a Cambodian village. I was sat beside the driver in the front of the car and had to turn to listen to her sat behind me. "Oh gosh!" she thought later. "I've just hammered this poor guy and made him twist his neck for three hours!"[2]

Rebecca wanted to know everything. How did we assess the capacity of foster families and under what conditions? She also explained a shift in emphasis in her organization's approach. They had hitherto sought to influence orphanage directors and fieldworkers. There were pockets of care reform at a grassroots level across Southeast Asia. Some "got it" and were adjusting their approach. They were in a period of transition. They were setting up day care centers and family support programs. They looked to reunite children with their families, to take them out of the institutions and return them to their homes. If that was not possible, they sought wider kinship care or foster families. They needed professional training and support. Others did not "get it" at all. We were asking the wrong people the wrong questions. It came down to money. The way to tackle the issue was at the source, at the level of funders and donors. So far, not a great deal of work had been done to educate donors and sponsors. Rebecca and her team were now doing that in her native Australia. Their approach was strategic and systematic and involved saturation donor education. They were tackling

---

1. Quoted in Williams, *Working with Street Children*, 111.

2. Rebecca Nhep (Joint CEO, ACCI, and board member, Children in Families), in discussion with Philip Williams, January 30, 2018.

the problem at the root. If they could influence the donors and divert funds into family-based programs, would SFAC be able to help provide the field-workers with professional training and support?

I did not need a sore neck to respond. This was music to my ears. I agreed at once.

Rebecca's background lay in international development and manage-ment. What she wanted for her team was professional social work insight and practical measures to help reintegrate children with families and society. Her organization, ACCI, is part of Australia's largest Pentecostal denomination.[3] ACCI's research shows that support for orphanages is deeply ingrained in Australian church culture. According to ACCI's figures, just over half of Australian Christians of all denominations are involved in international child sponsorship of one form or other. This may involve sponsoring community projects or it may be supporting children in institu-tions. Among Pentecostals, the proportion rose to over 60 percent.[4]

Many Pentecostal missionaries and fieldworkers were coming to see the need for proper systems and professional social work practice. Rebecca and her team spent around eighteen months with fieldworkers, helping them to understand the need for change. Then they set about convincing their denomination's development and mission agencies, then the national executive. For some two and a half years, they attended conference after conference, visited churches in all Australian states, getting the issue "on platform" so that it could not be ignored. They gathered case studies, shot videos—Rebecca's husband is a skilled producer—and marshaled their evidence.

"We threw the grenades out and got everyone concerned and upset," Rebecca said. "Then we listened and absorbed their questions and their anger."[5]

Rebecca certainly took some flak. "People said all sorts of things. I was awful, I was evil, an antichrist. 'You are taking God out of missions!'"[6]

People have said similar things to me. It is hardly surprising in in-stances where orphanages are used to serve an agenda other than the

3. Australian Christian Churches International (ACCI); see https://www.accimis-sions.org.au/.

4. For details of ACCI's findings, see Knaus, "Orphanage Tourism." Additional insights from Nhep, discussion.

5. Nhep, discussion.

6. Ibid.

primary needs of the child. Yes, spiritual concerns are central to people of faith and should motivate and shape our approach. Surely though, holistic, child-centered care should be our priority? Children belong in families, not warehouse-style conversion factories.

I'd heard that Rebecca could be quite hard and even abrasive in her approach. She railed against injustice like an Old Testament prophet. When I did hear her address a conference she was not at all strident, but very measured, marshaling facts to support her case. She told it like it was.

For many years the concept of residential care was so deeply ingrained in evangelical and Pentecostal mission culture that it needed a jolt to make people consider alternatives. The Christian missionary community was not going to listen to voices from outside. When secular agencies presented the case for family-based care as an alternative to the traditional residential solutions, they often did so in an aggressive or challenging way. It was counterproductive and put Christian agencies on the defensive. Such language, coming from outside rather than from within faith communities, was hardly likely to win hearts and minds. It was no surprise that some Christian agencies balked at the message. Here were secular humanists out to infringe upon their religious liberties. Yes, some did have ulterior motives, using orphanages as a convenient way to fund other initiatives, seeking to convert vulnerable kids who had nowhere else to go. Others genuinely cared for the children and had their best interests at heart. It was simply that they had no other models to refer to other than the residential institutions inherited from their particular Christian traditions.

Rebecca Nhep acknowledges unapologetically that her initial approach was direct and robust. She found that every orphanage director or every donor believes that they are the exception to the rule. Everyone else might be doing it for the wrong motives, but they themselves are acting out of altruism. An initial shock was needed to jolt them out of complacency. Now, after some six or seven years, Rebecca's tone is more measured. The tide has turned. Within some two or three years of her initial challenge, Pentecostal missionaries and fieldworkers began approaching ACCI for help. They had seen it for themselves. Agencies from other denominations did the same.

"The issue is not whether the message is hard-hitting," Rebecca says. "But the position of influence from which it comes."[7]

7. Ibid.

Rebecca and her team earned that position of influence. They have developed new policies and procedures, new ways of informing and engaging donors. ACCI is currently working with sixty-one institutions at various stages of transition. Some have already made the change from residential institutions to day care and support centers. They offer microfinance programs, vocational training, and support.

I left my initial encounter with Rebecca with more than a crick in the neck. I left with invitations to visit a number of missionary organizations to review their procedures and help promote the transition and develop good practice. Our work in Sri Lanka flowed from this. I was also able to introduce organizations to one another. I put Philip Barker and his team in Myanmar in touch with Rebecca and the agencies she worked with. It is important that we work together, side by side, assisting one another, using our combined skills and insights to achieve the best possible outcomes for the children. These were small beginnings, but I became increasingly aware that a global movement had begun. It was happening at a grassroots level, at government level, and across international agencies. Something had shifted. Things were beginning to change.

It's another working day in Leeds. I'm visiting a grandmother to assess her capacity to provide care for her tiny grandchildren. The tots are toddling around our feet as I speak with the children's social worker from Leeds City Council, Dan Hope. At this stage, I am still working for the Council's social services department and juggling unpaid work for SFAC alongside. I'm often asked how SFAC has been able to provide so much training and support to international organizations with little or no money available. My answer is that there is a cost to everything in life, other than the air we breathe. If anything is available free of charge, it means that someone down the line has paid for it. How did we make that happen? SFAC worked hard to gain funding in the UK from friends, contacts, and businesses to ensure we could remain afloat. Very occasionally this was augmented by a donation from a charitable trust or foundation. Mostly we kept going in those early days because we kept our overheads low. I worked from home to avoid paying office rent. I worked long and hard, often over seventy hours a week. I would come home from my day job with Leeds City Council and start on my work for SFAC. I would work late into the evenings and sometimes hear Brenda call, "Are you working again?"

I retained my income from other work in order to draw down less money from SFAC funds. It meant that I could pay my own airfares, offer training free of charge, and only ask the organizations I worked with for contributions to in-country costs. It was unsustainable in the longer term. My old boss Valerie Hales was surprised I didn't burn out.[8]

Dan and I both get out our diaries to arrange a meeting. We don't want to embarrass the grandmother by discussing the details there and then.

I ask Dan how he is fixed for a particular week.

"I can't do that week, I'm afraid. I'm in Uganda."

"Uganda? Really? That's interesting."

"How are you fixed the following week?" Dan asks.

"I can't do that week I'm afraid. I'm also in Uganda!"

Dan and I laugh as we discover a mutual concern for care reform in developing countries. Over a coffee a few days later I learn that Dan has a master's degree in social work. His first degree was in international politics and international history with some emphasis on development issues. He spent six weeks as a volunteer with CALM Africa. He remains in contact and has visited Uganda regularly since 2007 in his own free time. Dan put me in touch with Joseph Luganda, program manager at CALM Africa.

"Joseph's doing some significant work," he tells me. "You really ought to meet him. I'm sure he could draw on the expertise of SFAC to help with foster care and kinship care across Uganda."

Joseph took more convincing. He laughs that he fended off three approaches from SFAC before he agreed to meet me!

> I assumed they would be taking a Western approach. I thought they would apply principles and techniques that worked in Europe, America, and the Western world. They might misunderstand the African context and their approach may not transfer to our particular conditions and societies.[9]

Joseph says that in our correspondence we used terminology he associated with Western contexts. Only when we spoke face-to-face did he realize that the formal principles we described were already happening informally. Forms of foster care and kinship care were common and embedded in the culture. In African societies care for children whose parents had died or

---

8. Hales, discussion.

9. Luganda, discussion (February 2018).

who were unable to support them adequately was the responsibility of the wider community.

> You have to understand that community is key to Africa. Without community, Africa would not and could not exist. Society would collapse. It is not like Western countries where the family unit is the main base. Yes, there is the family unit of course, but here in Africa, it is wider than that—the community as a whole takes responsibility.[10]

It's vital to strengthen those communities and, at the same time, help develop support systems at government and local levels. Andy Williams recognized this. Born in Uganda and educated in the UK, he returned as a probation officer in 1996 and set up a football club for street boys which developed into a social work program. The project was rebranded as Retrak and I served on the board for several years, advising on issues around family-based care.[11]

Many children from rural areas were drawn by the prospect of an imagined better life in the capital Kampala. Andy even came across one family who believed that people greeted new arrivals with free cash handouts![12] The reality, of course, was far different. Children were drawn into street gangs, drugs, and prostitution. Ugandan street kids were known as *baiyaie* (wildcats), a derogatory term from the Idi Amin era. They were feral, they were tough, they were hard to handle.[13] Many died through casual violence, disease, and substance abuse. They were rounded up by the authorities when their presence became embarrassing. Andy remembers hearing how nearly 500 street children were removed from Kampala's streets on the eve of a US presidential visit.[14]

The Ugandan government, like many others, has since introduced more robust standards for residential care. Also, like many governments across the developing world, its resources are stretched and there are often gaps between policies and implementation. The Ugandan authorities have set limits on the size of residential childcare institutions and the length of time they spend there. Yet many faith-based orphanages still operate

10. Ibid.

11. Andrew has written a book about Retrak's methodology which is a recommended text on some social work courses. Williams, *Working with Street Children*.

12. Williams, *Working with Street Children*, 100.

13. Andrew Williams, in discussion with Philip Williams, April 7, 2018.

14. Williams, *Working with Street Children*, 89.

unofficially, in an unregulated and amateurish way. It is an approach Mark Riley describes as both "unskilled and irrational."[15] His accounts are as hair-raising as any told by David Servant in Myanmar. In Uganda too, many institutions employ recruiters to target the poorest villages. The way some orphanage recruitment teams work is completely scandalous. In Cambodia, Cathleen Jones even encountered one such team at a village funeral. A funeral can last for several days with extended family and friends coming from miles around. In this instance, the recruiters mingled with the crowds, ingratiating themselves, and offered payment to the relatives of the deceased mother to release her children into their care.[16] Imagine it from the child's perspective. You're grieving, you feel lonely, you're trying to take it all in amid the mayhem of a funeral of hundreds, and you see a stranger talking to your relatives about what should happen to you next! It's a disgrace.

Andy Williams has a lovely story from Uganda with the position reversed. Retrak began to find foster families for street boys using informal community networks. With the support of community leaders, church pastors, or village elders, individuals and families came forward to foster the street boys for limited periods. Patricia was among them. Each of her five children had died, three from HIV-related illness. All her grandchildren but one were cared for by relatives, yet Patricia volunteered to foster a street boy, Josiah, for a period of three years. "I have enough love for more," she told Andy.[17]

Things were tough for both Patricia and Josiah at first, but with the support and advice of social workers, they saw things through and soon began to encourage others to consider foster care. When Patricia passed away, something extraordinary happened at her funeral. Neighbors and friends paid tribute to Patricia and spoke of her selfless care for others, even though she had so little herself.

> At her request a relative explained the foster care scheme instead of giving a eulogy. After the burial two neighbors (one in his eighties) and a relative came expressing genuine interest in becoming foster carers. I wondered at the time whether foster care recruitment at

15. Riley, discussion.

16. Jones, discussion.

17. Williams, *Working with Street Children*, 110.

funerals of foster parents had been thought of before! Josiah was fostered by Patricia's cousin.[18]

No prize for guessing which funeral option I prefer!

Dan now works for SFAC. He always told me that one day he would work for the charity full-time. That day finally came in July 2017. For years he had given up his vacation time, working with SFAC without pay, helping with training and consultancy as our work spread around the world. Dan's contribution has been significant. Not only did it help spread the load but it enabled SFAC to develop and deploy additional services. With Dan working alongside me, on a voluntary level at first, I was able to extend the training services and also offer more advice on assessments and case plans. Dan is particularly good at this. I often tease him by calling him "Dan, Dan, the Care Plan Man"! Without an adequate care plan, tailored to the conditions of each individual country, each individual family, each child, there are more opportunities for things to go wrong. When assessing what particular plan or strategy is best for each child, we have to take the local conditions into account. What is considered "good enough" or adequate differs from country to country and often from region to region within individual countries? We don't advocate moving a child simply because their housing isn't up to Western standards. It has to be based on the comparable standard in the surrounding community. Dan and I can provide input on this from our social work perspectives. If foster care is the chosen option, it has to be made clear that it is by no means the simplest solution. The principle is easy to grasp, but to process it well becomes more complex as it involves working with people. Human beings are unpredictable! What works in one family may not work so well in another.

To work effectively there has to be proper training and preparation. There should be agreed standards for "house rules," what is or isn't acceptable in the family home. This applies just as much to a Cambodian village house on stilts with bamboo floors as to any other home anywhere in the world. We have to be clear that the foster family understands the implications and the weight of the commitment they are taking on. We have to protect children and ensure they are safe. We don't want to place children in an environment where they can be harmed, abused, or neglected. We must ensure that the child is safe from threats from the family, neighbors, visitors, or the wider community. Will the family be able to care for the child

18. Ibid., 111.

physically and emotionally? Can they afford to support an extra child? We have to be culturally relevant. In Uganda foster care placements through CALM Africa involve very poor people living in simple huts and shacks. They often live in a single room and have very limited clothing and equipment. Yet their living standards reflect those of other people in the area and they can provide safe, loving, and supportive foster care. All these issues involve close cooperation between host families and the social worker. We have consistently found that the techniques and professional measures we use are applicable and adaptable anywhere in the world.

SFAC is no longer just about raising awareness of the value of *substitute* families and finding those families for abandoned children. It is about *strengthening* families of all kinds. These can be a child's birth family, a foster or an adoptive family. It could be blood relatives or friends of the family. They are all families. They all need strengthening and support. In so many parts of the world, the wider community is the key to providing that support. The role of the social work team, then, becomes one of supporting families and the communities they live in.

There can be problems associated with community or wider kinship care. Fostered children can be exploited by relatives or community members, particularly in terms of domestic or agricultural servitude. This is unacceptable and measures must be taken to ensure that children are not exploited. At the same time, we have to take local practices and conditions into account. In a society like Uganda's, where 80 percent of people still rely on agriculture, there are expectations that all children should assist with chores. This is perfectly reasonable provided it is kept within acceptable limits. In some societies, there is an expectation that fostered or informally adopted children who are not immediate blood relatives should carry out more than their fair share. A host family will often send their own children to school whilst the foster child stays at home to help in the fields, to fetch water from the well, and carry out menial tasks. This is unacceptable and the solution is adequate training, monitoring, and support.

When people ask us about the British fostering system, they invariably ask about the payment foster families receive. Are these people doing it purely for the money? Support for foster families varies enormously across the countries we work in. Some organizations supply loans to help families set up small businesses, to rear pigs or chickens, set up kitchen gardens and sell their surplus crops. Others provide help in kind, such as donating rice or food parcels. In Cambodia, Children in Families pay a small monthly stipend, perhaps the equivalent of around \$30–40. It is sufficient to provide necessities and cover the cost of the extra mouths to feed. It is not a wage or a fee that might cause dependency on external aid. In Uganda, CALM Africa provides free health care and education to the foster child and other children in the foster family as a way of providing much-needed support. Grants, loans, or skills development training can help families set up small enterprises. Philip Barker in Myanmar reflects that these are not always the right solution: "not everyone is an entrepreneur."[19] There is no one fixed way. The way we support foster families must be culturally relevant and appropriate in each case. Joney Hup gives an instance of a woman who raised and sold a pig, a process that took a whole year, in order to save sufficient income to support an abandoned child.[20] That represents a considerable investment on that woman's part but was commensurate with her means and available resources. The solution depends on context and circumstances. A stipend can work in some places. In others, it can create an unhealthy dependency or become unsustainable without additional funding for the support organization. The key principle in each case is that it should be practical, achievable, and appropriate to the culture and living standards of the community.

One of the main problems is not lack of people wanting to be care providers but the resources required to enable them to do so. If funds currently tied into cash-guzzling orphanages could be released into the communities themselves, more children and families could benefit. If we rethink how we assist people to manage these issues, involve them in decision-making, identify and fill any gaps in their knowledge or skills, then together we can find better outcomes. Family-based alternative care for children has always existed in societies around the world. We can help it revive and thrive if we use our own skills to *assist*, rather than *help*.[21]

An example from Zimbabwe illustrates this approach, both for child protection and community support. Our good friend and supporter, Florah Gumede, tells how young children in African villages are sent to fetch water at dawn or dusk, often at considerable risk. Men often lay in wait at the riverbank or beside the wells to attack and abuse the children. By involving

19. Barker, discussion.

20. Hup, discussion.

21. Although the terms "assist" and "help" are synonymous, there can be a subtle difference. To help someone may imply that you do it *for* them, to assist them means that you do it *with* them, adding your skills and efforts to theirs.

the village elders and community leaders, the eyes and ears of the villages, the risks are minimized.[22] In the West, we do not fully appreciate the crucial role such elders have. Moses, Florah's husband, is a community leader with power not only to hear and arbitrate in disputes but to legislate on behalf of the regional or federal authorities. I had not fully appreciated this when asked to address an assembly of over 200 villagers and community leaders in a remote Zimbabwean village. Florah was highly amused. I was standing in the place where the accused would stand in a village court of law![23] Brenda was with me and has fond memories of those days spent in the Zimbabwean bush. Florah still laughs when she remembers when "poor Brenda" ran screaming from the latrine when a flock of bats, disturbed from their daytime slumber, flew out from the shaft![24]

In 2014 I presented a two-day training workshop on family-based care for twenty-nine social workers in Bulawayo. We then headed to the Lupane district near Victoria Falls. For some years Brenda and I had supported a primary school in the village of Dongamuze, providing porridge for 154 children under five years old. The children start the day with a simple but nutritious meal of porridge made from maize meal, cooking oil, and ground sugar. Some of these young children had to walk four miles to get to school in high temperatures, leaving home at 5:30 a.m. Prior to the Porridge Project, children fainted from hunger and several developed *kwashiorkor*, a form of severe protein malnutrition characterized by a swollen liver, ankles, and stomach. However, since the project took off, ill-health has been significantly reduced and there are fewer reported instances of *kwashiorkor*.

Many of these children lost parents to HIV-related illness. Most were living with their grandparents or extended families. It was the first time we had seen the project and, as Brenda mixed the porridge in a huge pot over an open fire, I noticed that the water was dirty. The porridge came out a murky gray color. I inspected the water source and was shocked to find a filthy pond, full of trash. Here was an example of a brilliant idea jeopardized by using dirty water, the only source of drinking water they had, at great risk to children's health. We arranged the purchase and fitting of a 5,000-liter South African JoJo Tank to supply clean, filtered water from another source some distance away. The tank is well maintained and

22. Florah Gumede, in discussion with Philip Williams, March 15, 2018.

23. Ibid.

24. Ibid.

the diesel pumps which drive it are kept replenished. Whenever I speak to Flora, I ask, "Are the pumps still running?"

"Yes, Mick," she laughs. "Those pumps are running fine!"

Flora started the Porridge Project. What SFAC brought was the means to identify and resolve the issue with the water supply. It was a joint effort and makes the point very clearly; it is all about *assistance* rather than *help*. It is also a practical example that means a great deal to some of our long-standing supporters. It represents child protection in more ways than one and a tangible outcome that people can appreciate and understand.[25] Kinship care and informal forms of community care for orphaned or abandoned children have been practiced in Africa for centuries. It can be strengthened with appropriate assistance and support.

When it comes to kinship care, Florah says that the key lies with the grandmothers. "Support the grandmothers and the children will be safe!"[26] She believes that there are ways of creating sustainable income so that more children can go to school. Supplying eggs to the tourist hotels around Victoria Falls is one option. As Retrak discovered in Uganda and as Brenda and I have seen in Zimbabwe, Ethiopia, and many other countries, there is "enough love for more." There is love to spare. The resources are harder to find. Where they do exist, they are often misdirected, siphoned off, or applied to the wrong things. They need to be redirected, to the villages, to the families, and to the people with the love to share.

25. Adrian and Delyth Burch (SFAC supporters), in discussion with Philip Williams, December 5, 2017.

26. Gumede, discussion.

11. Rescue to Restoration

ORDINARY FAMILIES LIVING IN LOCAL COMMUNITIES,
DOING EXTRAORDINARY THINGS.
—SFAC CORE PRINCIPLE[1]

ADDIS ABABA AIRPORT, JULY 2009. I shuffle along to my allotted seat, stow my baggage in the racks, and do what I normally do on a long-haul flight. I check the selection of in-flight movies and wonder when we'll get tea or coffee. I pay little attention to my surroundings. I have flown hundreds of thousands of miles. It's a chore. It's a bore. I stopped enjoying flying years ago. John Ellerington is more alert.

"Here, Mick. Have you noticed how many couples there are taking Ethiopian kids out of the country?"

I look up and scan the aisles. Almost every seat seems occupied by Western families, all with a black baby or toddler, all excitedly talking into their cell phones.

"Yes, we're flying out of Addis now . . . she's gorgeous. She's sooo cute!"

"Mom, Dad, we're flying out now. We can't wait to get him home!"

We later learn that this particular year saw the highest level of inter-country adoptions out of Ethiopia, many of them to the US. In 2010 the number of Ethiopian children adopted by US couples peaked at 2,500.[2] Ethiopia began to place increasing restrictions on international adoption until it outlawed the practice completely in January 2018. Until that point, it accounted for almost 20 percent of international adoptions by US citizens.

---

1. How SFAC describes the work of foster carers. It is one of our core principles.

2. For figures on international adoption from Ethiopia, see Joyce, *Child Catchers*, 134–35. In both 2009 and 2010 Ethiopia sent a total of 4,500 children abroad through international adoption; in 2010 some 2,511 of these went to the US.

From 1999 until the ban, some 15,000 Ethiopian children were adopted by Americans, including Hollywood celebrity Angelina Jolie's adoption of Zahara in 2005.[3] Dan Hope describes it as "the elephant in the room." It is a highly controversial area and one which has received widespread media coverage. It continues to divide opinion.

Let's face some more hard facts. If there is an orphanage industry and a voluntourism industry, there is also an international adoption industry. The scale is hard to quantify but up until 2009, there were an estimated 40,000 international adoptions a year. The Hague Convention on the Protection of Children and Co-operation in Respect of Intercountry Adoption set safeguards and standards for those states which ratified it.[4] The Hague guidelines state that where possible a child should be raised by their birth or extended family.[5] If this is not feasible, authorities should consider other forms of permanent family-based care within the child's country of origin. Article 21 of the UNCRC covers children's rights in circumstances of adoption. It recognizes that international adoption can be considered if "the child cannot be placed in a foster or an adoptive family or cannot in any suitable manner be cared for in the child's country of origin."[6] International adoption should not, under any circumstances, be undertaken for "improper financial gain for those involved in it."[7] Both the Hague Convention and the UNCRC agree. International adoption should only be considered after all national alternatives have been taken into account and then only if it is in the best interests of the child.

People often ask for my views on international adoption. I dealt with cases during my time as a social worker in Leeds. It is an issue I come across regularly in my work now. My answer is simple and similar to my views on residential childcare. When a child needs rescuing from a bad situation we should look beyond that immediate stage to the next, the restorative element. Any option is viable provided it is legal and is in the child's best interests. When considering international adoption, we have to ensure that

---

3. BBC News, "Ethiopia bans," line 19.

4. For a list of signatories, see: https://www.hcch.net/en/instruments/conventions/status-table/?cid=24. The US is not a signatory.

5. The text of the 1993 Hague Convention itself does not define what the "best interests of the child" are. However, its *Guide to Good Practice No 1*, published fifteen years later, does outline key factors to be considered, including the investigation of "national solutions first" and the principle of "subsidiarity" (see 2.1.1, paras. 46–53).

6. UNCRC, art. 21(b).

7. UNCRC, art. 21(d).

we have considered all the domestic alternatives. This is not about making financial comparisons or a simple economic assessment of relative standards of living. That simple equation has been used to justify many international adoptions. What are we saying if we call for the child to be taken out of poverty to a better standard of living elsewhere? That the child has been born in the wrong place, at the wrong time, and to the wrong parents? They may not enjoy as comfortable a lifestyle in their own country but they can be happy, safe, cared for, and loved. Too often we look through a lens of wealth and opportunity. We should look at it holistically, the advantages and disadvantages, the child's life prospects in comparison and context with other children in their country. We should also, of course, consider the law, and the law in many countries is clear. International adoption is a final resort and the child's culture, ethnicity, language, culture, and religion should all be taken into account. Unless there are good, solid reasons such as the provision of specialist medical care that might not be immediately available in the child's home country, then it should always be a last resort. Once again, the key issue has to be the best interests of the child.

How does this work in practice? What systems and procedures do we need to put in place to ensure that our approach is as child-centered as possible? The answer, of course, is that it is a multifaceted and multiagency approach. It involves the child's parents, if living, their wider family, their community, social services and health professionals, and the legal system. Crucially, of course, it also involves the child. That is the starting point. We start with the immediate needs of a particular child in a particular situation and we work outward from that to find the most appropriate solution. We don't start with the needs of an institution; how many beds do I need to fill to keep my children's home viable? We don't start with the needs of a church; how can we bring children to faith and raise the next generation of preachers and evangelists? We don't even start with the needs of a family; how can my abandoned nephew help me on the farm? We don't start with the desires of a couple overseas who may wish to adopt and add to their family or help a child in need. Rather, we start always and only with the needs of the child. Only then should we examine the options to find the most appropriate solution.

The United Nations Guidelines for the Alternative Care of Children recognizes the family as the basic unit in any society.[8] It may be a biological family, or an extended family or clan. It may be one made up of

---

8. UN General Assembly, Res. 64/142, "Guidelines"; FICE Youth, *Guidelines*.

children only, with older children looking after younger siblings. It may be a temporary foster family or a permanent adoptive family. It is still a family and still the ideal, as long as the child is safe, provided for, and loved. The core principle is that "children who cannot live with their parents should still grow up in a loving home and enjoy all their rights."[9] No institution, no matter how well-run or managed or well-resourced, can replace that.

Some believe that earlier research into the impact of institutional care on children has overstated the negative effects. They believe that whether care is provided through an institution or in a family context, the setting itself is less important than the quality of care the child receives. A three-year longitudinal group study by the Positive Outcomes for Orphans (POFO) research team, led by Kathryn Whetten, argued that earlier studies largely focused on extreme situations such as Russia and Romania in the immediate post-Communist period. At that time, most orphanages in these countries were large, hospital-style institutions employing shift workers.[10] Their own studies found little statistically significant difference in welfare indicators between children in orphanages and those in families. Even so, Whetten's report acknowledged that children raised in families had fewer reported emotional difficulties.[11] The study compared children in institutions with those living in vulnerable communities with unsupported families, rather than with families receiving assistance.[12] SFAC does not advocate children staying in struggling families without any assistance. Instead, we strongly insist that families are supported and strengthened so that the children receive the benefits an institution may provide, such as regular food and access to education, plus all the emotional benefits of remaining in a family. We know that the combination of physical and emotional care is far and away the best option, provided the child is safe.

What the POFO report does indicate is that quality of care is important and that we cannot assume that one form of care is intrinsically better than another. Even the best institution, however, cannot replicate the best family care. It cannot provide the same sense of belonging, identity, or connection. The emotional connection will always be lower in an institution

9. FICE Youth, *Guidelines*, 4.

10. Whetten et al., "Three-Year," see Introduction, lines 17–19.

11. Ibid., see Results, lines 32–35.

12. Williamson and Greenberg, *Families, Not Orphanages*, 14–15. Additional observations provided by Caitlin Lance Hope.

and Whetten's study illustrates that too. It is hard for any institution, of whatever size, to recognize a child's individuality. Dan often tells the story of how he noticed one boy in an institution he used to work in who had a particular liking for tomato ketchup. One day Dan put some on the table where the boy was sitting. The boy thanked him, something he was not in the habit of doing, and said, "Nobody's ever remembered I like tomato ketchup. Nobody's made this much effort before. It's nice to be treated like an individual!""

In one of SFAC's training exercises we ask participants to list what they see as both the advantages and disadvantages of residential care. Time and again, across all cultures and societies, we find they come up with the same things. The advantages are health care, regular food, a balanced diet, education, activities, a warm bed, friends, rules and structure, and routine. Some list safety, assuming, against all the evidence, that an institution will be safer for the child. If it's a faith-based group, they will list spiritual awareness and development. All very important needs and all can certainly be found within properly run institutions. Then we come to the disadvantages. We are careful not to prompt but allow the group to say what they think. Time and again, whatever the country, whatever the culture, their answers are the same: loss of family, isolation, loneliness, and lack of attention, warmth, and love. Some list loss of identity or sense of self, loss of culture or even language, social stigma, and loss of community.

These are seriously deep-rooted issues. Joney Hup says that there are over 360 distinct dialects within Myanmar. Yet, so often, children from tribal districts are sent to institutions in Yangon and other cities where their particular dialect is unknown.[13] They are culturally and linguistically isolated, separated from their home communities. Often the children cannot speak the same language as their peers or staff. Just think, if the child was able to return to their family and community after a number of years, how difficult would it be for them to communicate with those they love? I have seen this in almost every country where SFAC has worked. Take Uganda—there are strong cultural and linguistic differences between the north and south. The culture of fishing communities differs significantly from that of subsistence farmers or cattle herders. CALM Africa is mindful of these cultural issues when seeking to reintegrate a child into his or her

13. Hup, discussion.

community context.[14] Do residential institutions always pay similar attention to context and background? Not in our experience.

Bogotá, Colombia. A girl celebrates her eighteenth birthday in a state-run residential home. It is sparse and Spartan but she has plenty of friends. The staff present her with a birthday cake, they lay on a party. As the joy and laughter die down and the party comes to a close, the girl looks toward the door. Her suitcase is packed. It's waiting near the doorway out onto the street. Steve Bartel, a missionary with decades of experience working with street children, sees the look of terror on her face. What's more, he sees it in the eyes of her seventeen-year-old friends. They know that when their next birthday comes the same will happen to them. He vows there and then that he will never do such a thing to the children he cares for in his own family-centered homes.[15] I know Steve well. We've worked together very fruitfully over the years. Whilst he would never dream of doing such a thing, many people do. I've come across identical instances to the shocking example he cites, even recently in Colombia. The process of "aging out," of moving a young adult from alternative care to independent life, requires careful management and support. Such schemes are spreading across the world. In Phnom Penh, for instance, the M'lup Russey NGO provides an integrated aging out program to help young adults make the transition from care to independence.[16]

Young adults leaving foster care or residential homes can be isolated, vulnerable, and alone. They have little or no reference points when it comes to family life, to relationships, and the raising of children. They have no role models to follow nor networks to learn from or tap into for guidance. If they return to the residential home, they might be turned away or even not be recognized. You are an adult now. You can stand on your own two feet. In societies in which young people remain with their parents until marriage, they have no one to see them through that transition. They have no one to fall back on in times of trouble, no one to share special events with throughout the year.

Of course, nobody wants to close all residential institutions and turf the children out onto the streets or place them with ill-prepared or ill-equipped families. SFAC certainly believes that some specialist homes are

14. Luganda, discussion (February 2018).

15. Bartel, discussion (May 2018).

16. See http://mluprussey.org.kh/en/.

needed for children with special needs. The reality is also that potential foster families or adoptive families are harder to find for older children and teenagers. It is just a fact of life we have to deal with. No country in the world has yet found enough foster care providers because it is costly, emotionally and physically challenging, and often needs a succession of care providers. That process has to be managed and supported. If we close institutions down too quickly, how do we know that the family alternatives are safe? It needs proper monitoring and evaluation, proper professional support. This applies equally if children are reunited with their birth families or provided with foster homes. Some governments have acted hastily in implementing the recommendations of the UNCRC. We have heard horror stories from countries where children have been removed from institutions without adequate or appropriate alternatives. In many countries, governments have introduced legislation designed to curb and regulate the proliferation of large hospital-style institutions. This is a positive move, but a size limit can sometimes be set which makes it difficult for smaller, more family-style institutions to register.

Smaller residential institutions can often act as transitional bases leading toward family or kinship care. Bureaucratic processes can slow or hinder the deinstitutionalization they are intended to promote. Policies intended to help can end up being counterproductive. It is important that care providers work with their local government authorities to ensure that the officials responsible for implementing policy understand the issues involved.[17] Both SFAC and most organizations we work with believe these problems are temporary. The overall trajectory worldwide at a policy level now favors family-based care. The key to turning policy into reality lies in implementation through dialogue, collaboration, training, awareness, and education. That is why SFAC has put so much emphasis on engaging with national and regional authorities, the judiciary, and professional social services. When those responsible for legislation and policy decisions for child placement understand the issues and the various forms of alternative care, real progress takes place. Equally, when charities and NGOs demonstrate that they can be trusted to deliver childcare services responsibly and professionally, the greater the opportunities for lasting change. I regularly tell the leaders of the NGOs I work with, "You have to earn the right to sit at that table. You have to earn the right to sit in city hall and for your voice to be heard. You have to demonstrate that your program works, is effective

17. Steve Bartel, in discussion with Philip Williams, January 30, 2018.

and delivers." I am always thrilled when I hear from a mission agency or secular NGO that their regional social services department has approached them for assistance and advice. They are showing that it works.

In Latin America, a mother comes home to find her teenage son having sex with a street girl the family had taken in from a rescue mission. The girl had been a sex worker, exploited and abused by successive men. The mother is understandably shocked and upset. Her initial reaction, in her shame and confusion, is to blame the girl. I am careful in my response to blame neither the girl nor the woman's son. This girl had known nothing but exploitation and abuse. Perhaps she responded to the boy's attention in the only way she knew? There are serious issues of safety in an instance like this, for everyone concerned. For the host couple, their children, the neighbors, the school, other children in the community—and of course the girl herself. This is why social work input is so important. The process from rescue to restoration must be managed professionally.

Everyone likes a spectacular rescue story. What we don't so often applaud are the stories of restoration—the slow, steady efforts that make a difference. Steve Bartel tells how many of the earnest young missionaries who work with his organization want to be in downtown Bogotá, confronting drug dealers. They want to hear the wail of police sirens, feel the adrenaline rush as they intervene to save a child. Not all of them appreciate the slow recovery, the step-by-step process of nurturing and care that goes on unseen and unsung.[18]

"Ordinary families living in local communities, doing extraordinary things," is how I describe the foster caregivers I've seen in the UK and so many places around the world. It has been my privilege both to help train and prepare them and also impart my own knowledge and skills to others so that they can do the same. It has also been a privilege to work alongside other organizations to devise means to support these people during this most demanding of roles. Caring for someone else's children is never easy. It often involves making stark choices, tough decisions.

Kampala, Uganda, September 2011. Dan and I are conducting training for CALM Africa volunteers. Dan has already delivered sessions on child protection. Now we are considering care plans and methods of assessment

---

18. Bartel, discussion (May 2018).

with social workers and volunteers. One of the volunteers tells us that there is a child nearby, shut into his home all day.

"Come on," Dan said. "We've had the theory. Time for practice. let's go and find out more, see what the child needs. We can develop a real-life care plan."

I thought I had seen it all by now, but nothing had prepared me for what I saw when we reached the child's shack. I was shocked. The boy was about six years old, frail, skinny, completely naked, covered in sores. He clearly had learning difficulties. He was sat in the dark on a single sheet on the mud floor of his shack, locked in with no food, no clothing, just a bowl of water.

"Where are his parents?"

"We don't know," the neighbors tell us. "His father is away somewhere. His mother works in town, she's a hairdresser. She locks him in each morning when she goes to work until whenever she returns home."

Dan and I assisted the volunteers to obtain the information they needed to make an informed decision on how to help the child. They asked appropriate questions of the neighbors and the mother when she arrived home. Has he any siblings? How often does she leave him? Where does she work? Can someone pick her up and bring her home? Where is the father? Does the child play with other kids in the neighborhood? We listened to what was said and made suggestions on the sort of questions to ask. There was so much to consider. Together we addressed the issues layer by layer to agree the best options for the child. Local knowledge, the insights of neighbors, and community leaders, the skills of professionals—all combine to provide an appropriate solution. We assisted in asking the right questions. The community and the CALM volunteers provided the answers and continuing support. It was a powerful, real-life case study of community-based childcare in action. And it made a profound impression on us both.

On another occasion with Joseph Luganda in December 2013, I encountered a child-headed household for the first time.[19] The eldest boy was about fourteen. He had three siblings aged ten, eight, and six. Their home

19. Households headed by children first came to international attention in the wake of the HIV/AIDS crisis and in conflict zones. The issue is much broader and more complex. Some children live this way because of parental neglect, perhaps through alcohol or drug abuse, or because their parents have mental health issues or are absent for extended periods. In some instances, they may choose to remain on a particular plot or patch of land, however meagre, as it is the only asset they have. Insights from Luganda, discussion (May 2018).

was broken down and almost derelict. Razor-sharp corrugated iron sheets teetered precariously from the roof. It looked as if it could collapse at any moment. The boy was covered in sores and bites. He scavenged for root crops in the fields each day in exchange for a few coins. He and his siblings slept on the earth floor which oozed with mud when it rained. They had no matting, no pots and cooking utensils, no lighting. They did not go to school.

"Their father is a drunk," the neighbors told us. "He's away somewhere and rarely visits. Their mother has mental health problems. She cannot care for them. We don't know where she is."

It was then I felt it. I felt what all my training, experience, and knowledge told me was wrong. I felt as I would have felt years earlier, before my studies, before my social work experience, before SFAC.

Get these kids out! Find an orphanage. Find someone overseas who can adopt them. Someone in North America, Europe, Australia, anywhere! Just get these kids out of this dreadful place! That was my first response, an emotional one. It was fleeting but it caught me off guard. It was one of those moments when I could fully understand the reactions of an orphanage director. This child needs help. I've got an orphanage. Problem solved. These situations tear at your heart. Brenda suggested we adopt a Brazilian girl when we returned to the UK in 1998. It was a lovely thought. I entertained it briefly in my mind. But no, that wasn't the solution. That wasn't the way to proceed, not in Brazil, not in Uganda either. As drastic as the children's plight undoubtedly was, there had to be another way. As Joseph Luganda explained from his deep understanding of the Ugandan context, "Mick, if these children leave their home they will lose it straight away. It is *their* home. It is the only one they've got. If they go to an orphanage or into foster care, they will be separated. They won't only lose this plot of land. They will lose one another."

It felt raw, it felt harsh, but this was the right thing for those children. We all took a deep breath and began to discuss a care plan.

Joseph Luganda will tell you that if siblings are separated, as they so often are by the orphanage system, they will live hundreds of miles apart. If one of them dies, they will be buried apart from their loved ones, they will be buried alone. In Ugandan culture it is a terrible thing for families to be buried separately. How much worse, then, for children placed indiscriminately in institutions, with no records of where they've come from, no record of their community, no acknowledgment of their particular culture or home?

Joseph will also tell you that many child-headed households want to remain together. They do not want to be fostered, adopted, or placed in an orphanage. They want to remain together in their own home, however meager it may appear. These children are vulnerable. They are open to exploitation and abuse. Neighbors or relatives may oust them from their home or tiny plot of land. They want to stay put.[20] A care plan must recognize that. We have to be ready to think outside the box and develop a culturally sensitive and appropriate response. The formal systems of family-based care we have in the West don't always do that.

We had trained the CALM Africa volunteers and now we observed and assisted them to complete an assessment and devise a care plan. The children needed matting for the floor, repairs to the walls and roof. They needed pots and pans, lighting and gas. They needed oversight and people to check up on them to ensure they were safe. We found people in the community who were prepared to look in on them and prepare them meals. CALM Africa runs a school and there were places there for the younger children, although the eldest refused. The solution was local, it was community-based, it was African. I later heard that Joseph and his team met the children's father and they were able to resolve complex issues with relatives on the ownership of the land. For a few hundred British pounds, we kept a family intact, preserved their identity, and protected their home.

20. Luganda, discussion (May 2018).

12. Putting Children First

TO BE INSIDE THE SFAC MIND IS TO BE INSIDE
THE MIND AND EMOTIONS OF THE CHILD.
—TONY HODGES[1]

BENGAL, INDIA, 2014. CAITLIN Lance[2] is working in a small residential children's home when she learns that two British guys are on their way to brief and train the staff. As an Australian psychologist specializing in child trauma, she is aware of the debates raging back home about the harm institutions can inflict on children. She's heard the word "evil" bandied about and understands how it could apply to the giant, soulless orphanages she's seen and heard about. She understands that some are run purely for profit or for ideological reasons, to influence or convert children. Strong terms like "wicked," "exploitation," and "abuse" may certainly apply to some of those places, but not *this* one. The staff are so committed, so caring. Visitors are signed in and out. There are robust procedures in place to protect the children. Besides, it's a relatively small institution, only twenty-six children. That's tiny compared to some of the huge warehouse-style orphanages found across India.

This is not Caitlin's first visit. Back in 2010, at the start of her doctoral studies, she spent a fortnight here with the Christian charity World Vision. She observed aid workers in action and tried to understand the culture and the issues around poverty, HIV, drug addiction, and family separation. After returning to New South Wales, Caitlin worked with an NGO dedicated to helping asylum seekers and people suffering from torture or trauma.[3]

1. T. and V. Hodges, discussion.
2. Now Lance Hope
3. Service for the Treatment and Rehabilitation of Torture and Trauma Survivors

She is well qualified, experienced, and very cognizant of the disputes over the appropriateness of residential childcare in developing countries. To address her concerns, she began her six-month placement with six weeks of observation so that she could better understand the day-to-day running of the orphanage. Caitlin wanted to understand how the place was run before drawing any hasty conclusions or starting therapeutic interventions without fully understanding the context. She soon realized that she was not best placed to deliver therapy. The placement was too short, the issues too complex. Instead, she could help the staff to understand some of these issues. It was not her job to provide therapy but to create a therapeutic environment. Also, working through interpreters, who were often members of staff themselves, she realized that the children did not always want to open up to her in front of staff they saw every day. They withheld information that they might otherwise share had the interpreters not been involved with the institution itself. Caitlin knew the set up was not ideal but had profound respect for the love and dedication the staff showed the children in their care. Now the home's supporters in Australia were telling them that they had to deinstitutionalize. Now, these two British strangers were coming to tell them they were doing it all wrong.

The training session lasted four days. Caitlin acknowledges that she entered it very defensively.

> I was very much open to the concepts I knew that Dan and Mick would bring but protective of the team—as children's homes go, it wasn't a bad children's home. I knew these people I was working with—they were good people—they poured their heart and soul into caring for the kids. Whilst I was on board with the message of deinstitutionalization, I was all for going to the training session and saying, "Look, these are good people and you need to back off!"[4]

Caitlin says that by the afternoon of the first day's training she realized her fears were unfounded.

> By the end of day one, there was a real sense that Mick and Dan were in this *with* people. They had worked in residential care. They'd been on this journey. They weren't there to judge, they were there to give us new information and to talk about how we could change things. For me, this represents a key strength of SFAC.

(STARTTS). See http://www.startts.org.au/.

4. Caitlin Lance Hope in discussion with Philip Williams, June 5, 2018.

They are not there to tell you that you'd been horrible. They were not there to hammer in the mistakes we'd all made. They were there to support us. Yes, we did the best with what we knew. Now we knew differently; how could they help us to implement that?[5]

By now Dan and I were in the early stages of developing a system of remote support for the organizations we worked with. We knew that we could only scratch the surface through a few days' training. Caitlin was educated to doctoral level. She was already familiar with many of the areas we covered in our training sessions. Yet she appreciated the opportunity for ongoing support in an area outside her expertise. Within days she had sent an email to Dan asking for help with a particular issue and another to myself. The correspondence continued. We pointed her toward information and resources.

Dan and I both knew that we were introducing concepts to people who often had no specialist training or background in childcare or development. We also knew that many of these people were reeling from the realization that they might not have been doing things the right way. Through ongoing remote support, we could help them both to understand the issues and to deal with the often-painful adjustments they were making to their ethos and practice. In Caitlin's case, she was working through issues she had seen for herself. Our role was to help her to do that.

> Our particular home was billed as one for children suffering from trauma and neglect from physical or sexual abuse. Some of the children did come from high-risk backgrounds. Others had nowhere else to go. For the most part, though, most of them did have homes and families. Given proper support, those families could have continued to look after their own children. I worked with one particular child who had experienced abandonment, neglect, and inconsistent care from the various adults in her life. Her face was often devoid of emotion. She would sometimes shut down completely when under stress, sometimes to the point of curling into a fetal position and becoming unresponsive. I realized that I didn't do nearly well enough to incorporate other staff into that work. I became the focus of the child's attachment. I did not prepare the child for the transition to other care providers. The focus should not have been on my relationship with the child but on me as the support person, someone who facilitated support from the care providers themselves. That was a real challenge and it caused me

---

5. Lance Hope, discussion.

to see the value of what SFAC does. It is all about strengthening relationships. With attachment trauma, the most significant healing comes from core relationships, not with the supporters, the social workers or psychologists, but the care providers. If we can strengthen and support them, the attachment difficulties can be resolved.[6]

As a psychologist learning about social work practice Caitlin had a thousand and one questions. She wanted to know how to process, interpret, and apply these concepts to the work she was doing. She was accustomed to developing plans for her work but not for the child's everyday living. This was as new to her as it was to her colleagues in the home. Caitlin observes that without the follow-up support from Dan, the changes would have taken place a lot more slowly and less extensively. Without that support and without Caitlin pushing to implement change, the lessons from the training sessions may not have become embedded and followed through. Together, we had begun to weave another strand into the services we provided.

SFAC was evolving. We were moving with the needs of organizations. We had shifted from advocacy and initial consultancy to training. Now we were offering continuing support. We were no longer only saying *why* childcare must change. We were helping organizations understand *how* it must change.

I was with Dan and Walter in Uganda when Caitlin showed up. Before we flew over, Dan mentioned in passing that someone would join us during our visit but not who it was. When I asked who it might be, he told me it would be Caitlin.

"Caitlin? How come?"

"It's just that she wishes to learn more about SFAC and how we work."

"Okay, that's good. Where is she staying?"

"Same place we are."

"So, who's funding it?"

"She is."

"And who's arranged it all?"

"I have."

"Dan—is there something I should know?"

"Might be."

---

6. Lance Hope, discussion.

My social worker's observational skills were way off beam on this one! I had no idea!

Caitlin had decided to break her return trip to Australia via Uganda, not the easiest or most sensible logistical arrangement, by any means! She took advantage of the opportunity to visit some other organizations and to continue her conversations with Dan. It was their first official date after talking for eight months online. Walter was also quick to take advantage of her visit. He was about to deliver a training session on child development and attachment.

"Look, it seems odd me running this when we have a psychologist present," he said. "Caitlin, do you fancy running this one?"

Caitlin did so. She enjoyed it. The session was well received. The SFAC team was about to expand.

Dan proposed to Caitlin during her visit to the UK a few months later. I often joke in training how SFAC's commitment to strengthening relationships and families reached a new level. We had become a marriage agency! I was delighted. My work was bringing people together in more ways than one! Also, Caitlin's involvement brought something extra and very special to the range of services we could provide. Caitlin trained as a clinical psychologist in Australia, registered as a chartered psychologist in the UK, and has additional qualifications and experience in anthropology, education, and training. She has strong academic and research credentials, practical field experience, and invaluable insights into how it feels to be on the receiving end of SFAC's training and support. She understands the kind of organizations we seek to help, the challenges they face, the right way to present things to them, and how they might respond. Most importantly of all, she knows what it means to get inside the mind and emotions of a child.

For many years, people assumed that SFAC had a large and complex team behind it. I used to joke, "You looking for SFAC? 'Tis me!" There was also Brenda, with her top-notch administrative support, as well as trustees, friends, and donors. It was hard work, passion, and commitment that kept us going. If a bank charged high transfer fees for converting UK donations into local currency around the world, I would protest.

"Look, I've got a faithful old lady who sponsors us to the tune of £5 a month. Are you telling me that you're going to eat into that by levying a transfer fee?"

We ran a tight ship. We fought our corner. It was hard graft. It was the only way to offer the support required by those organizations who would otherwise struggle to afford it.

Ashlee Heiligman, of Global Child Advocates, remembers that when she first worked with SFAC in Thailand, she looked us up online to get a sense of the scale and scope of the operation. She was surprised to find how relatively small we were, both in terms of personnel and donor support. Yet she recognized that what we offered was something different, a body of knowledge and expertise that could be "poured into" and shared with other groups in a way that they could make their own.[7] Dan jokes that our aim is to share our expertise with others so that they themselves become experts in their area and, in so doing, work ourselves out of a job!

In a parallel way, that is also how we work with orphanage directors. I reassure them that there will be more than enough community work for them to do once they start to reunite children with their families or find them foster homes. They won't lose their jobs, rather their jobs will refocus and change. With training and support, they could become community workers, people who strengthen families and find safe homes for children. The big question is, are they up for it? Are they prepared to develop their skills, learn more about the work they are involved in or do they just want an easy ride and stay as they are? I tell them that I faced exactly this situation in England. The residential home I worked in had begun to take on fewer children. My country's policy toward residential care had changed. Institutions were closing in favor of family-based care. If I didn't undertake some kind of training, I would have been out of a job.

SFAC has now developed into a multidisciplinary team. It is no longer just about Mick Pease and what he can bring to the table. It's about a group of professionals passionate about children and doing the best we can for them. We now have a team that is a mix of social workers, psychologists, trauma therapists, lawyers, and the tireless administrative team that keeps it all going. We all bring something to the table. We all have a part to play in providing care for children. Yes, social work is the key ingredient. But we also need the skills to understand children's emotions and behavior, how we support parents and carers to look after children effectively, and how the law can support us to place children in safe families.

7. Ashlee Heiligman (executive director, Global Child Advocates), in discussion with Philip Williams, April 24, 2018.

The role of how important lawyers are is best illustrated for me by Ranjit's account of a case involving a child from Uganda. I have seen Brazilian judges moved to tears and Ranjit himself choke up as he relates the story. It was a complex case involving family separation, visas, and a potentially simple solution in the form of fostering by a British family. Ranjit probed deeper. During a training visit to Uganda, he looked up the boy's family and established the full picture. Through his tenacity, dedication, and by exploring every possible legal avenue, Ranjit was able to reunite the child with his mother and wider family. He has wonderful photographs of the occasion when they were reunited. He tells the story to illustrate how everyone involved in the process had to agree and define what was in the child's best interest. That is the key principle in all we do. It's no longer all about "substitute families." It's about training and advice on care plans and care recording, on child protection, on strengthening and supporting families. It's about understanding child development and psychology, about creating a therapeutic environment, about understanding how children and families function.

Tony Hodges puts it this way:

> To be inside the SFAC mind is to be inside the mind and emotions of the child. Institutions are about need-meeting infrastructures, about physical and social provision, about avoiding deprivation.[8]

Institutions will only take you so far. A family is all about a network of relationships. The SFAC family is the same. We complement and augment one another's skills, perceptions, and personalities. It is not only about our technical skills but a shared conviction, vision, and ethos. Neither is it all about templates and models, although we certainly do deploy those. Dan describes it as having "set knowledge, but no set model." In fact, he tells me that the thing that first attracted him to the charity was that there was no model![9] What we do have are the required knowledge and skills required by practitioners in our fields. We are all qualified and trained in our particular disciplines and are experienced in working across cultures and borders. It may sound obvious but it is worth saying, the professional skill sets are crucial. So is an appreciation of the context. This means understanding the particular circumstances that apply in each case with each individual child.

8. T. and V. Hodges, discussion.

9. Dan Hope, in discussions with Philip Williams, December 5, 2017, and June 5, 2018.

The same applies when dealing with different organizations and cultures. An appropriate model should be applied in each case. Yet why do we still see mission agencies or aid relief NGOs applying the same identikit models the world over? There's a crisis. Quick, open a children's home! Put in a few bunk beds, some toys for all the children to share. No consultation, no questions asked. Such checklist responses can do more damage than good. It's a complex world that requires a nuanced response. Tick-box assessments simply won't do. That is why SFAC supports organizations to develop and apply critical skills.

SFAC works *for* rather than *with* children. Caitlin and Tory Barrow can help establish systems to facilitate therapeutic support. Ranjit offers his legal services, pro bono, to provide training and advice on child and family law. Dan, Walter, and I all provide training and ongoing support. As far as we know, we are unique in providing training across the three disciplines of social work, therapy, and child and family law. We believe that to best serve vulnerable children, child protection systems require expertise in all three areas. We are all passionate about what we do. When delivering training I sometimes have to pause for a moment. I become emotional about the problems children face. I have long since stopped worrying about getting upset when explaining a child's hurt. I was raised with the expression, "Boys don't cry." Well, I can tell you, they do and they should! Men do feel that pain and should be encouraged to display that from time to time. It isn't a sign of weakness but of strength. Passion and professionalism go together.

People often tell me that it is my own story and experience that resonates with audiences. We all respond to personal stories, and relate to ups and downs, failure and success. I speak about my time as a residential social worker, the lessons I learned from the confrontation with Eddie and from many other challenges I faced. Our training sessions can be very interactive and often emotional because they trigger memories among workers and volunteers who spent time in institutions or were abandoned themselves. There are times of tears and times of laughter. Walter Young remembers a training session in Iraq where he played the role of a child in institutional care being told something he didn't want to hear. He got so involved that he cowered under a table as an Iraqi woman playing the role of a social worker tried to coax him out. At this point the door flung open and the regional head of social services marched in with an entourage of officials plus TV cameras come to see how the session was going. They all stopped dead in their tracks as Walter peered up at them from under the table![10]

When I started to travel with SFAC, I quickly realized that as well as advocating for change, I needed to contribute to it by equipping those who listened with the knowledge and skills to make it happen. So, I began to train them. I developed my style of presentation and delivery in the field. I had to work with whatever was at hand. There were often large bottles of water or water dispensers where we trained. I used them to illustrate how it might feel to be an abandoned child, hovering between home and the large institution. I straddled the space between the bottles. This large bottle is the orphanage, that small bottle is the child's home, that one the village, that one an aunt's house in a nearby town . . .

People enjoyed the sessions. They liked the interactivity. I've found this particularly apparent in former Communist countries. Dr. Ruth Barley lectures in sociology at a British university and works with the Romania International Children's Foundation (RICF), an NGO committed to strengthening families and child-centered care.[11] Ruth says that her multidisciplinary social work and child psychology team warmed to SFAC's training. They were used to knowledge delivered from "on high," largely by a powerful male acting as if he knew all the answers. Interactive training that was both informative and fun was something very new to them.[12] Ashlee Heiligman describes other training sessions in our field as "passable" and informative but sometimes lacking the passion and practical application SFAC prides itself on.[13] She also believes that it helps those trained to equip others. Those we train can then pass on the baton to other people, to share what they have learned. It's the ripple effect. I cite it a lot in training. Equip the messenger and they will take that message far and wide. It can reach places we never knew existed or are unable to visit ourselves. In Brazil in 1998, I dropped the first pebble in the pond. Today, two decades on, the ripples are still spreading ever outward.

---

10. Young, discussion.

11. Fundația Internațională pentru Copii, România; see https://www.ricf.net/.

12. Ruth Barley, RICF team in discussion with Philip Williams, May 29, 2018.

13. Heiligman, discussion.

13. The Lonely in Families

A FATHER TO THE FATHERLESS, A DEFENDER OF WIDOWS IS GOD
IN HIS HOLY DWELLING. GOD SETS THE LONELY IN FAMILIES.
—PSALMS 68:5-6A

STEVE BARTEL WAS BORN in Colombia at the height of a civil war. His parents were missionaries. They returned to the US when Steve was thirteen and he later returned to the country of his birth. For four decades, Steve and his wife Evi have worked as missionaries in Colombia. In 1987 Steve and Evi took in a family of seven abandoned children. They ranged in age from twelve down to just ten months. Had the children been placed into government care they would have been separated. Back then, the Bartels applied a model that was gaining currency as an alternative to large, impersonal institutions. They had small farms where children could live in family-sized groups. The seven children were cared for in three family units. The Bartels rented a house for the children's grandmother so she could live close by. They all lived within a mile radius of one another, attended the same school, and saw each other regularly. Some of the children were eventually adopted by other members of the missionary team. Steve and Evi adopted three other children themselves.[1]

The Bartels have walked the talk. They know the reality of fostering and adoption; the challenges and the joys and heartaches of taking on someone else's children. Steve has a wealth of stories and colorful analogies from his forty years' experience of mission work. He uses one to illustrate an important point about fostering or any form of alternative care. He's known people ask if he has room for a dog on his farm. They fell in love

1. Bartel, discussion (January 2018).

with a puppy which soon outgrew the available space. He chuckles that, however large, a Saint Bernard stays cute and cuddly for life, but a full-grown Doberman is quite another prospect.[2] Whether it's a cute baby or an abused teenager, we are talking about human beings who grow, who change and develop. We should consider the longer-term implications, for all involved.

Street kids are invariably exposed to violence and abuse. It's often the only life they have known. They follow the behavior patterns they have seen, copy and perpetuate the abuse that's been inflicted on them. It takes time and careful nurturing, not only to take the child off the street but to even have the chance to take the street out of the child. Even in less extreme cases, where children may not have been "wildcats" or "disposable ones" like the street children of Uganda or Brazil, a stigma can attach to those fostered or in care. A recent study of children and young people in foster care in the England found that some felt "labeled" or patronized by special treatment. They simply wanted to be treated "like a normal teenager."[3] The child's integration into family life and the wider community must be managed as naturally and seamlessly as possible. Careful recruitment, training, preparation, and support are crucial.

In SFAC we know that when families come to foster, they are more likely to want younger children, from babies up to eight years old. It is far more difficult to find foster families for teenage children, those with disabilities, behavioral difficulties, or street children. We also know that younger children require stimulation, interaction, and attention which is much more likely to occur in a family setting than in an orphanage. SFAC always used the strap line, "Children belong in families." We adhere to that still. It is our watchword, our guiding principle. But it doesn't stop there. "Children belong in *safe* families," is the pertinent point. That is where the full toolkit comes into play: the social worker, the child psychologist, the lawyer, the trainer. Allied to all of that comes the provision of practical support and resources to enable families to care for their own or other people's children. We are not alone in that; other charities and NGOs offer this too. Take RICF, for instance, the NGO Ruth Barley helps run in Romania. Their core values and principles[4] are almost identical to ours. I

2. Bartel, discussion (May 2018).

3. Narey and Owers, *Foster Care*, 120.

4. Children belong in loving families; Protection from harm; Child-centered care; Integrity and Justice; Unity and Diversity. These are all values that resonate with my

am sure they resonate with donors and supporters. What can be more difficult, however, is getting supporters to understand exactly what is needed to put these principles into action. Ruth says that potential supporters can entertain two equal and opposite misunderstandings. They may assume that things remain unchanged from the Communist era, or they may think the problems are all resolved.[5] The days of giant Romanian orphanages may be over but vulnerable children and young adults still need support. RICF runs its own fostering program and offers support and training to foster placements funded by the Romanian government. It supports young people in full-time education beyond the age of eighteen and provides ongoing life skills training for independent living. People are often surprised by the range and depth of support services offered by organizations like RICF. Surely, it's all about homes and institutions? Of course, the reality is very different. It's about tailoring services to address particular needs. People who grew up in government care often lack the documents they need to claim financial support. Teenage mothers are often expelled from school as bad examples and lose out on education and training. RICF helps in these and other instances.

These are the sort of holistic issues that many of the organizations we work with seek to address. They aren't dramatic. They don't fit the gung-ho "rescue" narrative that many associate with charity and relief work. Yet they are essential services that can make all the difference. Both Ruth Barley and Philip Aspegren will tell you how donors are happy to fund *buildings* and *plant*.[6] Here's a truck we sponsored. Here's a medical facility. You can see pictures of it online. It is less easy to enthuse people to fund psychologists and social workers, legal aid specialists, and counselors. People don't readily understand why they are needed and what they are for. When asked about her work with Burmese migrants and refugees in Thailand, Ashlee Heiligman often finds that people are interested in the dramatic rescue aspect. "How many teenage sex workers have you taken off the streets?" When she starts to talk about the prevention, family strengthening, and community support work, they begin to lose interest. Two decades since I ground my teeth in frustration at the apparent failure of relief and development organizations to appreciate the need for social workers, the problem

colleagues.

5. Barley, discussion.

6. Barley, discussion; Aspegren, discussion.

persists. People remain sadly misinformed. The ripples are spreading but in terms of public awareness and perceptions, we have a long way to go.

"So, Mr. Pease, what do you think of our orphanage?"

I grip my cup of tea and grasp for an answer. I don't want to offend the matron, a prim Roman Catholic nun. I'm in Sri Lanka and about to deliver training for The Sisters of the Good Shepherd. Before the session starts they show me around. It's clean and comfortable but very austere, very institutionalized. The girls share showers, there is little privacy, large dormitories, locked doors, barred windows. I sip my tea. I don't want to offend my hosts but neither do I want to approve of what I've seen.

"There are other ways of providing care," I say, tactfully.

"I know," says the nun. "That is why I've invited you here to share with us."

I breathe a sigh of relief. We can talk candidly.

The nuns invited me back to deliver a further session the following year. I hear very encouraging recent reports. They run community initiatives to protect and empower girls and young women on the tea plantations. They run short-term hostels and family reunion and reintegration schemes.[7] They have turned good intentions into good practice.

When I first set up SFAC, I sat down with my son Mark's father-in-law, John Casey, to discuss strategic direction. John worked for a statutory body in the UK so I figured he would have a handle on these issues.

"Mick, can I ask you what success would look like? How would you measure the success of your work with childcare organizations?"

I struggled to think of an answer that might sound erudite enough.

"If they ask me back," I quipped.

That might not be as flippant an answer as it sounds. SFAC have been invited back many times in many countries, as in the case of the Sri Lankan nuns. We have never once canvassed for work overseas. All the opportunities have come through connections we've made, by word of mouth or recommendation.

In Sri Lanka the Atkinsons introduced me to their government contacts. I went from province to province training social workers and probation officers. In some areas, the entire regional social work teams had the day off to attend. We trained all officers involved in reuniting children

---

7. Narel and Alison Atkinson, in discussion with Philip Williams, April 24, 2018; Alison Atkinson, in discussion with Philip Williams, May 8, 2018.

with their families. My words were translated directly into both Sinhalese and Tamil to ensure everyone understood. There is no room for ambiguity when you are dealing with children's lives. The government set targets to close residential institutions and either return children to their families or find family or community alternatives. This process requires careful management. To implement such a policy everyone involved has to understand its importance and be equipped to carry it out. The issues are complex. There may be incomplete records about a child's family or home community. There may be little evidence why the child was separated from their family. Where there are adequate records and one or more surviving parents, it is obviously much easier to get children home. Where there are no problems with safety, then the authorities can work with children and families to develop appropriate care plans. The Sri Lankan government decreed that residential institutions should have no more than 5 percent of children with one or more living parents.

Many residential institutions reunite children with their families only to recruit other "orphans" to replace them. "Look, there's the exit door but here's the entrance door." Instead, they should begin the process of awareness-raising and assessment, the sort of work Joney Hup does in Myanmar and Joseph Luganda in Uganda. They visit families and assess how and why the child came to be living in the institution. They find means to support them when their child comes home. Unless we address these issues, there is a risk of emptying children out of orphanages and onto the streets. Sri Lanka revised its targets once it became apparent it could become a "numbers game." Caseworkers competed with one another to show how quickly they could comply with legislation. I am told that the Sisters of the Good Shepherd now go further than government targets. They refuse to take any child with a living parent.[8] They have put the structures and systems in place to do so. It's not an issue of numbers but an issue of quality. It's about improving the skills and awareness of all involved so that the right solutions are found for each child.

The process of deinstitutionalization that began in the larger residential homes has spread to the smaller, family-style units. In 1997 Philip Aspegren and his wife Jill moved from the US to the Dominican Republic to set up group homes for abandoned or vulnerable children.[9] These were smaller, family-style units, similar to those Steve Bartel developed

8. A. Atkinson, discussion.
9. Aspegren, discussion.

in Colombia. Walter Young and I saw similar village-based arrangements in Croatia. We had our reservations but they were preferable to the large, impersonal institutions. A missionary couple and their children might take in perhaps eight to ten local children and bring them up together in their home. A network or close-knit campus of perhaps eight to ten homes would then develop, sharing resources, farming land, engaging in small business enterprises. It kept families together.[10]

For all the advantages of this approach, the Aspegrens gradually realized how institutional it could become. All the eight-year-old boys would receive the same presents at Christmas or birthdays, rather than something that was unique to them. The Aspegrens were also surprised to find 95 percent of the children in their care had living biological parents. Every so often one or other parent would turn up on campus to visit their children.

"We saw that we were not running an orphanage at all, but a boarding school for families in difficult situations," Philip Aspegren remembers.[11] With that realization, the adjustments came.

I visited some projects that operated this model during my field research in 1998, notably ABBA,[12] run by Thomas and Susanna Smoak not far from São Paulo. The Smoaks had seen a similar arrangement with college-aged youths in Honduras. They set out to create a similar initiative based on five properties in Brazil. Thomas remembers how the "belonging" element was missing from this model and how the eight or so boys living with surrogate parents were not accepted by the other children in church. Although the children were far less institutionalized than those in the large orphanages, there was still a stigma attached. Thomas noticed how this changed as the children moved to a foster care model. Then the children were regarded as part of the families and not as strangers from an institution.[13]

Thomas later invited me to run some training sessions for his team. We developed a three-phase approach. An initial "rescue phase" followed by a transitional period where the child's needs were professionally assessed. There followed a family-unit houseparent phase until such time

10. In some parts of the world the term "foster care" can be used to describe this type of group home model. As this book makes clear, SFAC applies the term to duly authorised and supervised family-based care for children who are unable to live with biological family members.

11. Aspegren, discussion.

12. Associação Brasileira Beneficente Aslan.

13. Thomas Smoak, in discussion with Philip Williams, January 15, 2018.

as the child could be reunited with their biological family, if possible, or placed into a foster home with ongoing support. This was groundbreaking in Brazil at that time. The juvenile judge for São Paulo State cited Thomas and his team at ABBA as the only group to be implementing foster care in the entire region, an area with a population of some 45 million.[14]

ABBA is well regarded. They had some fifteen years of faithful and effective service. They worked well with the local authorities. Thomas acknowledges that he overcame an initial and irrational mistrust of sociological mechanisms and what he took to be "secular practices." With my help, he came to regard these as good practices and entirely commensurate with this work as a missionary. He appreciates the theological as well as the professional basis for our work. He is impressed that we share the same theme verses from Psalm 68: "GOD sets the lonely in families." This expresses SFAC's core values and founding principles. We link it strongly to issues like family reunification, safe substitute families, and adherence to the UNCRC.

When the regional authorities received a grant from the Italian government to train social workers in foster care, they approached Thomas to find out how it was done. When he appointed a Brazilian social worker to carry out professional assessments, Thomas introduced her to the regional social care officers. He remembers them pouring out of their office building to greet them and to give the newly appointed social worker an ovation!

"At last, Pastor Thomas has appointed a social worker!" they cheered. "Now we won't have to read his endless reports!"[15]

I returned to work with ABBA many times. He remembers how his team looked forward to my visits and how our interactive training sessions were engaging, informative, and often very moving and fun. We quickly developed a rapport. He translated for me and laughs as he remembers how we both "got in the zone," drawing on one another's passion and enthusiasm, sharing a rhythmic "call and response" delivery like two old-time Pentecostal preachers![16]

Thomas arranged for me to address the local judge, social workers, and psychologists. As we left I was horrified to hear him issue a general invitation for them to attend a training session I was running for potential foster families the following Saturday. I protested that the training requirements

14. Smoak, discussion.
15. Ibid.
16. Ibid.

for each of these audiences would be very different. A single session could not possibly meet the needs of both. In the event, only one of them turned up, Vania, the head psychologist for the region. I was worried she'd find it very basic but she joined in all the exercises and not once revealed she knew more than anyone else. She thanked me at the end of a full day and invited me to address her students at Ibirapuera University where she coordinated the psychology course.

"Say exactly what you said today, only in a condensed version," she told me. "You have ninety minutes. There will be about thirty students."

I arrived at the University and was surprised to find they had canceled all the evening classes for all of the five year groups on the course. The entire faculty would be there to hear me, some 200 students.

Vania explained that they wanted them all to hear about my practical experience of family-based care, child development and attachment.

"They know the theory but never hear the practical applications." Once again, I found how much the message I carried was needed in Brazil.

Thomas observes, "Mick will likely be remembered as the father of foster care in Brazil. His trainings have helped all of us at ABBA learn how hard and rewarding and right it is to help families and kids live together."[17] ABBA now has full certification from the Brazilian government and can draw down state funding to assist with its programs. As far as we are aware, it was the first family strengthening and foster care NGO program in São Paulo State to establish a formal partnership with the Brazilian authorities. Thomas, his coworker Delton Hochstedler, and myself had created something substantial, something that has now matured and continued. We had pioneered foster care in a city of twelve million people, in a Brazilian province with a population roughly equivalent to that of Peru or Venezuela.

On August 3, 2009, the Brazilian National Congress sanctioned Law 12.010 to "guarantee the right to family life for all children and adolescents." The new law stipulated that if residence with the natural family was impossible, children and adolescents be placed with guardians or adoptive parents, or into time-limited residential care. The longest any child should stay in residential care was to be no more than two years.

All over the world, governments began to draw up legislation in line with the UNCRC. In Cambodia and Uganda, in Thailand, Paraguay, and

17. Thomas's endorsement appears on our brochure, "Turning Good Intentions into Good Practice"; see http://sfac.org.uk/wp-content/uploads/2018/05/SFACPartner-Brochure.pdf.

Brazil, laws and standards set limits on the size of residential institutions and the time children should spend in them.

The tide has turned. It has turned at government and judicial levels. It has turned within many institutions, and many mission and development agencies. Philip Aspegren is optimistic about the future. Currently, Casa Viva is the only NGO in Costa Rica to run family-based childcare programs. Yet he is convinced there is an "unbelievable opportunity" for faith-based and secular children's homes to become transitional bases for family reintegration, deinstitutionalization, and community-based care.[18] Ashlee Heiligman also makes the telling observation that anyone who sets up an orphanage now is going to have to face displacing the children sooner or later. All over the world, many governments are phasing out residential homes. Why set up a new one only to have to go through the process of deinstitutionalization at some point in the near future? Why not start wherever possible with family-based alternatives from the outset?[19] The challenges we now face are the low level of public awareness of the issues, particularly among donors and supporters, and the need to resource, fund, and support family-based alternatives. Together we can face and meet that challenge.

SFAC's work spans three core dimensions—past, present, and future. We help preserve the child's identity—*the past*. We aim to create a safe and stable *present*. We plan for a secure *future*. These concerns are universal. They apply to all cultures and societies. The first particularly resonates with cultures and religions which stress the importance of family heritage and context. It is equally applicable within our more individualistic Western culture. We need to know and understand our roots. The second and third are fundamental to the child's current and future well-being. A safe and secure family provides the bedrock. It is in the best interests of the child, of the community, of society as a whole.

18. Aspegren, discussion. Philip estimates that there are around 125 residential institutions in Costa Rica accommodating between 2,500 and 3,000 children.

19. Heiligman, discussion.

14. The Connections Continue

SHE CANNOT EVEN REMEMBER HIS NAME.

A VOLUNTEER COMES FORWARD. I place the end of the string in their hands. We are about to start one of the most powerful and emotional group exercises in the SFAC toolkit. I unravel the ball as I move to the next participant in the circle. One volunteer represents a child, the others each represent a person in that child's life. It could be a parent or relative, a school teacher or social worker, an orphanage director, a mentor or friend. No one has to speak; they simply have to stay in place and hold the string. We try to be careful when choosing a volunteer to represent the child at the center of the circle. We know it can have an emotional impact. The string indicates connections to relatives, friends, the wider community, formal and informal support networks. It illustrates the complex web of links and networks involved in the care of a vulnerable or abandoned child. Soon the room is crisscrossed with string, starting with family then moving out to schools, community groups, government agencies and NGOs, even supporters and donors, all represented by the participants. We then begin to show what happens when changes take place. The child may move to a new care home or foster family, a source of funding may dry up. I cut the string to represent a connection lost. I may connect the loose end to another participant to indicate a new connection only to sever it again. Many children experience loss after loss. The important people in their lives drop away one by one. As the relationships cease and the connecting string is cut, the child is left with a handful of trailing loose ends. If they are lucky, they may have one or two remaining connections, but all the others have been lost. The child is left with rejection and so many unanswered questions. They are on their own.

This moment in the group exercise always has an impact. For the first time, people involved in decisions that affect children's lives can see the devastation such losses cause. It often reminds them of their own pain if they themselves were let down. As a trainer, I often find myself fighting my emotions, holding back the tears. The volunteer holding the loose strings represents many thousands of children experiencing separation and loss. Sometimes, after a few quiet moments of reflection, someone will say, "That child was me! I know how it feels." Others will say, "I was in a position to help but I let that child down by not supporting their cause." These are always powerful moments; when the emotional impact brings home the practical knowledge we have already introduced and worked on.

I remember powerful moments from other exercises. A subsequent group exercise we call "A Child's Origins Are Important" can have an equally powerful effect. During an ABBA training session in Brazil, we learn that Tony, one of the participants, has just one memento of his childhood; a thumbed and faded photograph of himself as a baby. He has no record at all of his biological family, where he started life, or how he ended up in an orphanage—nothing to pass on to his own children. The exercise comprises twenty questions about childhood memories. Tony can answer only one. The photograph is all he has. Yes, the nuns were kind. They seemed to care. One day, he returned to the orphanage he once thought of as home.

"Remember me, Sister? I lived here for years. I'm doing alright now, I've got a job—I'm working with orphans and street children."

The nun smiles, "Should I know you?"

She cannot even remember his name.[1]

We all know how important relationships are. In family life, we gather collective memories, of our grandparents or even older ancestors. We are rooted in a context, a time and place. Relationships are the channel for our past, our present, and our future. A secure family base, or the closest approximation that can be found, is crucial for those channels to work. This is what provides us with context and meaning; somewhere we can call home, somewhere we can celebrate anniversaries, holiday seasons, weddings and ceremonies. Children need support to flourish into young adulthood and beyond. These vital networks and relationships can prepare them for a secure future.

---

1. Discussion.

We encountered no ideological objection to family-based care in Brazil. Its culture and society is warm and caring. There is a tremendous emphasis on community and family life. The issues were easily identifiable but far harder to resolve: how to link theory with practice; how to engage the all-important judiciary; how to overcome certain cultural misconceptions over the management of the attachment process. Jane Valente, of the Brazilian child protection service SAPECA[2] in Campinas, remembers the period from 1997 to 2001 as "muito tensos" (very tense). Social workers convinced of the desirability of family-based alternatives sought to convince the state authorities. Some considered the proposals risky at best, downright "louca" (crazy) at worst! Only in 2005 did the foster care program become a recognized service within Brazilian public policy.

> Mick's visit to Campinas brought hope and his practice encouraged the professionals. Since then, his presence always brings a word of trust, a shared experience. Whenever he comes to Brazil, he tries to dedicate a little of his time to us, bringing his knowledge to professionals and families. We are grateful for that.[3]

Relationships are the key to progress. Every time. Thomas Smoak and ABBA began working in Brazil in 1992, initially with street children, although the remit has since widened. Before I met them briefly in 1998, Thomas and his team were already reuniting children with their families and trying to introduce foster care in an informal way. When I met him for the second time in 2006, I asked how things were going and he told me about the difficulties. The biological children of foster families often reacted badly when a foster child arrived. The street children were so traumatized and had so many problems that speedy integration into family life was impossible. I asked if they had ever considered advance training and preparation for foster carers. This was the start of a long relationship. For ten to fifteen years, I delivered training for small groups organized through ABBA, then larger groups, regional groups, countrywide groups. First, there would be ten to twenty people, then a hundred people with a waiting list of another seventy. Eventually, I was addressing groups of up to 400.[4] Delton Hochstedler takes up the story:

2. Serviço de Acolhimento e Proteção Especial à Criança e ao Adolescente.
3. Statement from Jane Valente, trans. Delton Hochstedler, May 4, 2018.
4. Recollections augmented from materials provided by Delton Hochstedler.

> What has been interesting to see is how the work of SFAC has joined together with a societal shift here in Brazil. SFAC has been a part of that but has also pushed that along, to move from taking care of children in institutions to taking care of children in families. Because of that, SFAC's training was not only useful to the families; it was also useful to the professionals; the psychologists, social workers, and judges—both at a high court level and a lower court level. So, all sectors of society have been involved, learning and understanding the specifics of how you take care of children in families.[5]

Delton will stress that a particular concern was to avoid mistakes made in the UK as it went through the process of transitioning from residential to family-based care. British practitioners did not have all the answers but we could impart our own experience. Both Brazilian foster families and social workers could then avoid the pitfalls we faced along our own journey. The training covered the basics. What is foster care? What do foster families do? How can they prepare their own families to receive a foster child? How do they manage the process of "letting go and moving on"? How could they prepare themselves for the time when the child would pass from their care into another foster home or back to its biological family? This proved to be a particularly pertinent issue in Brazil, for specific cultural reasons.

I met Bel Bittencourt in December 2014 at the 3rd International Colloquium on Foster Care in Campinas. Dr. Edson Luiz de Oliveira, then Judge of Childhood and Youth in Bel's district, invited me to present a three-day event in May 2015. I later returned to participate in a state-wide childcare conference. Bel remembers me demystifying a popular belief about fostering in Brazil, that temporary attachment causes undue emotional harm. This belief had long hindered the widespread deployment of fostering services.

> Mick described attachment as a good thing for a child's development . . . Today we know how important building secure bonds is to the cognitive, social, emotional, and brain development of children, especially those who have suffered trauma in early childhood. The foster family has a critical role in encouraging healthy bonds and once the child learns to attach, he or she may become attached to other people.[6]

5. Delton Hochstedler, in discussion with Mick Pease, audio transcript.

6. Statement from Bel Bittencourt (social worker in São Bento do Sul), trans. Delton Hochstedler, May 7, 2018. For the theoretical basis, see Bowlby, *A Secure Base*.

Through a foster or substitute family an abandoned or vulnerable child develops a sense of trust and connection. They become better equipped to form and maintain closer relationships in the future. A good foster family bonds with the children in their care. Likewise, the child may attach to the foster parents and mourn their loss as it moves on to a new foster home, to its own family, or into adoption. The pain of separation can be intense on both sides. Just as the trauma of separation occurs in the context of relationships, so does the process of healing and restoration. The process needs to be managed carefully. Caitlin observes:

> In the vast majority of cases, the day-to-day interactions in the context of relationships with reunited parents, foster parents, or other key carers are more powerful and effective than any professional therapeutic relationship. This means supporting the carers is absolutely essential![7]

I was delighted when Delton passed on some feedback from a foster family in Brazil. They wept as the child moved on but thanks to their SFAC training understood that it was in the child's best interests for a brighter future.[8] What Bel Bittencourt calls "the culture of foster care" developed gradually in the UK. In Brazil, Bel and her colleagues are at the forefront of that development.

I must have visited Brazil over thirty times. On one occasion, I flew in and out and back in again within a matter of days to meet briefly with social workers and other professionals! I often say that if a call comes from Brazil, I will drop everything to respond. Wherever else I have been around the world, I return to Brazil again and again. To borrow a phrase from my own social work discipline, I've developed an attachment to the country; to its social service and legal professionals, its professors and lecturers, its families, its children, its people. In order to follow things through, to bring family-based care to fruition, I became "part of the journey" for those I train and work with. They became part of my journey too. Delton Hochstedler, a clinical social worker specializing in child trauma, now coordinates ABBA's technical team. Delton acts as my interpreter and has developed his own contacts, credentials, and standing. It's the ripple effect again. The connections continue.

7. Caitlin Lance Hope, email message to Philip Williams, February 19, 2018.
8. Hochstedler, discussion.

Asunción, 2012. It's my first time back in Paraguay's capital since Brenda and I visited friends there back in 1997 when our time in Brazil came to an abrupt end. I'm meeting Anja Goertzen Gaona, a children's legal advocate and missionary with the Viva Network and now Action International. Anja had met Susanna Smoak at a conference in Brazil and mentioned her interest in foster care. Susanna recommended SFAC and I subsequently received an invitation. Anja introduced me to social workers, government officials, aid workers, and missionaries.

One day, Anja told me we were heading five hours out of Asunción to the Mennonite colonies on the flatlands. The Mennonites are a Protestant group with origins in sixteenth-century Netherlands and Germany. In the 1920s and 1930s, Mennonites from Canada and Russia settled in Paraguay and other South American countries. They gained a reputation as effective and industrious farmers, tilling the soil others preferred to overlook. To my surprise, Anja told me we were going to meet and encourage foster families. She explained that the Mennonites had practiced informal fostering for years, generally from within their own communities in cases of parental death or marital breakdown. They might occasionally take on children recommended for care by the judicial courts. I addressed a group of around forty or fifty in a church hall and asked how many were fostering children. A substantial number raised their hands. Once again, informal family-based care was already happening. Our role was to strengthen and encourage them. Paraguay is a small country, just six million inhabitants. Family-based care is not yet as developed there as it is in Brazil and some Central American countries, but it is advancing. It is easier for a small country to adopt changes and to adapt quickly. According to Anja, there are encouraging signs in Paraguay with multiagency collaboration at all levels, between governments and NGOs, between Catholics and Protestants. As in Brazil, SFAC works with the government and judiciary. During my first visit, I was offered an audience with an English-speaking children's judge in the Supreme Court of Paraguay. He gave me half an hour to explain why I believe family-based care is best and how successful it can be.

In March 2017, Dan and I gave presentations in the Supreme Court to between 200 and 300 people. SFAC has hosted a Paraguayan delegation in Leeds, just as we have done for groups from Iraq and other countries. At the time of writing, we are due to be visited by a second delegation from Paraguay. Dan will then return to Paraguay with Ranjit and Nigel Priestley, a family court lawyer, to train legal workers. On the final day of a hectic and grueling schedule, we met a regional judge imagining we'd wind down with a chat over coffee. Instead, she immediately whisked us into a room of around fifty delegates for another full day of presentations and training! Where there's a willingness to listen and engage, we will deliver every time.

In Brazil, Dr. Deni Luis was certainly prepared to listen and engage. At the foster care colloquium in Campinas, I addressed some of the main sessions and led smaller breakout groups and seminars. Dr. Deni, a children's judge, approached me after one session and invited me to discuss the issues I'd addressed. Although my Portuguese is sufficient for everyday conversation, I require an interpreter for detailed and technical discussions of this kind. With Delton translating, he asked question after question. The following year I visited him in Camapuã. I trained some of the court judges and their technical teams and he introduced me to the president of the Supreme Court of Mato Grosso do Sul. Together, we signed a declaration to place family-based care as the priority response for children in care in Mato Grosso, Brazil's third largest state. Later, Delton sent me a translation of an unequivocal letter circulated to the entire judiciary.

> With the advent of Law 12.010/09, known as the Adoption Law, and following what is already in Article 227 of the Brazilian Federal Constitution, Brazilian legislation added to the Child and Adolescent Law words of singular clarity decreeing that "the inclusion of the child or adolescent in foster care programs will have preference over residential care." In spite of this, while other developed countries already use this model of care, Brazil continues to institutionalize its children. Because of this, and in light of the legislative innovations, it is necessary to correct many decades of institutionalization of our children, determining that, when the child is removed from their family of origin, they should stay with another family that has been selected and trained for the task, while awaiting a solution for reintegration or moving to adoption, maintaining institutional care as a secondary solution as recommended in the law.[9]

The letter went on to mention training SFAC delivered in Camapuã and placed the justice department squarely in support of foster care with support where possible. Brazilian courts have a crucial role and the more

---

9. Oficio.n.163.629.073.0012/2015 Presidencia, Tribunal de Jusitiçia, Poder Judiciario do Estado de Mato Grosso do Sul, November 12, 2015, trans. Delton Hochstedler and emailed to Mick Pease, November 15, 2015.

judges and magistrates understand the advantages of family-based alternative care the better. Delton and the ABBA team tell us how appreciative they are that SFAC engages with the judiciary. We help the legal professionals understand how care planning and support for children in care. What systems and procedures should be put in place to manage the process? What are the legal timescales and what care orders are available? How do we determine if or when the child can return home? How can judges direct that process without being drawn into direct supervision, a drain on valuable judicial time? Like many NGOs and also Brazilian provincial and federal social services, ABBA also focuses on prevention as well as cure. How do you prevent a child coming into care in the first place? What can be done to assist the child's biological family? How can we tackle and alleviate poverty and deprivation?

There are currently some 47,000 children in social care in Brazil, a country with a population of 200 million.[10] This compares with some half a million children and adolescents in some form of care in the US, around 415,000 of them with foster parents. In England, with a population of almost 54 million, there are around 72,000 children in care on any given day, the vast majority of them outside institutions.[11] In comparison with England and the US, Brazil's figures may sound like a small beginning but the momentum is underway. Brazil is an enormous country. It comprises twenty-six states, all with varying laws and procedures. It is understandable and inevitable that progress would be slow and steady, even after the government passed Law 12.010 in 2009. Today, some nine years after the law was approved, only some 5 percent of children and adolescents in social care are in foster families. The remaining 95 percent are in residential institutions.[12] The task remains enormous. Yet change *is* happening. Care reform *is* gaining ground.

Words can't convey how delighted I am about the progress made in foster care and family strengthening in Brazil. The greatest progress has been made in the south of the country. The municipality of São Bento do Sul, in Santa Catarina State, implemented a foster care service in 2002 even before the legal provisions were in place. It remains the priority as

---

10. Figures translated by Delton Hochstedler from official Brazilian government sources. See http://www.brasil.gov.br/cidadania-e-justica/2017/06/governo-lanca-campanha-para-reduzir-numero-de-criancas-em-abrigos (in Portuguese).

11. UK Government, "Children's Social Care Data."

12. Bittencourt, Statement.

an alternative care measure to this day. Santa Catarina is currently the Brazilian state with the highest number of foster services.[13] Isa Guará summarizes the progress and challenges for the further development of foster family programs in Brazil.

> We have seen quite a lot of progress . . . but our numbers are still very small compared to the number of institutional care services in place. The highest quality foster care experiences are in the south of the country and Mick has traveled in several regions doing lectures and courses that mobilize public agents to move forward in the implementation of foster care services. From a political point of view, the issue is on the agenda of governments and agencies, and it is likely that there will be a significant increase in such services in municipalities, which will require more training and guidance from government officials and families. In the future, what seems to have a lot of acceptance is "subsidized custody," a form of family care within the child's own family, with resources and investments so that the uncles, grandparents, cousins, and other relatives take the children with more support and care services. However, this will require the intense social work of preparing and supervising the extended families included in this type of service. This, in addition to expanding the network of foster families, is a future challenge.[14]

Isa also envisages the development of services and programs for "those who age out of care until the age of twenty-five, as we have seen in European and Eastern European countries."

Slowly and steadily, foster family programs are gaining ground in Brazil. The vision planted during that conversation with Baroness Cox and Sam so many years ago is being fulfilled.

13. Ibid.
14. Guará, Statement.

15. Onwards and Upwards

I NOW KNOW YOU EITHER DO THIS WORK PROPERLY
OR NOT AT ALL.[1]

I LOOKED IN THE mirror and was greeted by a toothy grin. I had two front teeth missing. Two gaps, as black as coal pits. I was not a pretty sight. My dentist had removed two teeth that were beyond repair. He told me I'd need implants and that they would take considerable time to bed in. Time I did not have.

"I'm flying over to Brazil in a few weeks," I told him. "I can't go looking like this!"

I was due to address the judiciary and their technical teams at the Supreme Court of Cascavel. There were to be representatives from all over the region and beyond. How could I turn up without two front teeth?

My dentist offered a temporary arrangement. He could offer me some plug-in dentures. They would fill the gaps until such time as he could fit the permanent implants. When I tried them out later, I didn't know which was worse, the gaps in the top row or the prominent denture pegs that drew even more attention to the problem. When I tried to speak, my voice came out a toothy, sibilant lisp. In desperation, I emailed Delton for advice.

My heart sank as I read his reply. "Mick, there is no other nation on earth that puts as much store on dental hygiene and cosmetic dentistry as the Brazilians."

Great, thanks Delton. That's so reassuring to hear.

John Ellerington was my next port of call. I could always rely on him as a sounding board. He could listen and absorb whatever I threw at him.

1. Feedback from a delegate at the SFAC and Retrak workshop, "Specialist Training in Foster Care," January 2007, quoted in Williams, *Working with Street Children*, 109.

Whether from a draughty call box in Birmingham or a cloak-and-dagger powwow in a trailer in the Yorkshire Dales, Ellerington was my man. I arranged to meet him in a pub.

"Now, John, what d'you reckon? Are they better in or out?" I bared my teeth with the two dentures in place, then removed them to reveal the two gaping gaps. John laughed so much he fell off his bar stool and ended up on the floor. I could see I'd picked the right man to ask!

"What are you doing, Mick, go naked, au naturel?" he laughed helplessly.

It hardly needs saying that I was more nervous than usual when I got up to address the assembled delegates and dignitaries in the Supreme Court. I could see row upon row of delegates across the auditorium; lawyers, magistrates, social workers, government officials. They were all smartly turned out. I imagined they all had impeccable teeth. I took a deep breath and felt the intake of air whistle between the gaps in my top jaw. I launched into my presentation.

At the close of the event ceremony, as the applause died down and the organizers proposed a formal vote of thanks to Ranjit and myself, a small girl came forward to present me with a certificate. She must have been about eight or nine years old with a wide, enchanting smile. The conference delegates laughed uproariously when we smiled for the photographs. They gave us both an ovation. Like me, she had almost two identical gaps in her teeth! It remains one of my favorites among the dozens of photographs I've accumulated over the years.

I received feedback later that week. I was told my presentations were well received and understood. They loved the detail of the "British approach." One comment in particular remains with me. A delegate was overheard observing to a colleague, "Such passion! This guy must be so convinced of his message to get up and address an audience with his front teeth missing. I wouldn't do it!"

Passion and conviction will take us a long way. That applies to almost any cause or issue. Even when speaking through an interpreter, if you are fervent about what you believe, people will catch that immediately. I tell my story and present my case. Ranjit says he is always struck by how quickly I win an audience's attention.

> I look out across the auditorium and, within three or four sentences, Mick has them transfixed. He's got them eating out of his

hand. It's clear they don't all understand English, but even through an interpreter, he's able to make a connection.[2]

Ranjit believes that it's because I clearly speak from experience and use examples people can relate to regardless of culture or language. Everyone understands the story of Eddie.

Passion and conviction can attract attention, but they don't guarantee results. A quirky gap-toothed grin or dry Yorkshire humor, will only take you so far. To gain traction, an authentic message has to be shown to work. It needs the support of sound professional practice.

I offer a few reflections and suggestions in this final chapter. It's a call to action, an appeal for us all to ensure we inform ourselves about the issues that motivate us most. Good intentions, in themselves, are not enough. Most of those involved in childcare are generally trying to do the right thing. They may simply lack the professional skills and background to address the issues properly. In an area as delicate as child development, this can be disastrous.

In Uganda, Andy Williams drew upon SFAC to assess, recruit, train, and support foster families. Together, we hosted the first regional training in foster care in an event that attracted twenty-five delegates from five African countries. A female delegate left one of the most encouraging and significant pieces of feedback SFAC has ever received.

> I realise now we are not ready to launch a foster care program. This work is too precious to do poorly. You have taught me what it means to be professional and I know now you either do this work properly or not at all.[3]

Precisely. She did not go away and set up a foster care program. She did not go on to reunite families like Joney Hup in Myanmar or the Atkinsons in Sri Lanka. She did not set up a model program of quality fostering and family strengthening like Thomas Smoak and Delton Hochstedler in São Paulo or Cathleen and Dale Jones in Cambodia. Rather, she realized that a foster care program was not the right thing for her group to launch at that time. They would be better off playing to their own particular strengths. I would rather people realized that foster care was not for them and devote their energies to some other worthy cause than create an unsafe foster care

2. Ranjit Uppal, in discussion with Philip Williams, December 5, 2017.

3. Quoted in Williams, *Working with Street Children*, 109.

program. "This work is too precious to do poorly." We are dealing with children's lives.

SFAC is not the only NGO operating in this field. There are many others. Where appropriate, we share conference platforms, information, and insights. We all share common goals. Yet there are areas where we believe the SFAC approach is different and distinctive. For instance, not all care reform agencies trained potential foster families *in advance*. That has always been our policy and Philip Aspegren says it's this aspect of our model that appealed to him most. Once participants know what's involved they can either walk away or follow things through. They can make an informed decision.[4]

Here are some principles we hope you will find helpful. Some are professional points around good practice. Others are more personal, derived from our experience of running a not-for-profit organization with a global focus. We trust that these might be useful for both general readers and practitioners alike.

Stay Informed

Very often the response to the needs of vulnerable or abandoned children is based on good intentions rather than good information. Even today, many people are unaware that there has been a global movement for over sixty years in favor of family-based rather than institutional care. Caitlin recently alerted me to the results of a 2017 opinion survey by Catholic Relief Services that highlights a shocking lack of awareness among those surveyed.[5]

- Some 87 percent of the 1,000 Americans who participated in the survey believed that orphanages are common in the US today, even though they have largely been phased out over the last half century.

- Although most respondents recognized that residential institutions in low to middle income countries largely receive support from charities and religious organizations, some 42 percent did not understand the difference between a traditional orphanage and a group home.

- More worryingly from a care reform perspective, 60 percent said that they would consider providing financial support for an orphanage

---

4. Aspegren, discussion.

5. Catholic Relief Services, *American Perceptions*.

overseas and close to half (47 percent) agreed that they would prefer to give money to an orphanage rather than support a family living in poverty.

- Around half of the respondents assumed that orphanages are a cheaper and more cost-effective form of childcare than family-based alternatives. The opposite is in fact the case.[6]

Share the Facts

Although care reform is a growing, grassroots movement worldwide, there remains a lack of public awareness of the issues. Some 45 percent of participants in this survey incorrectly assumed that most children in orphanages are there because their parents are no longer alive. Few identified that poverty is the number one reason that children end up in orphanages worldwide.

I'm told there's a Chinese proverb which says that the more we know, the luckier we are. I had to know and understand child development theory in order to develop my social work practice. In a similar way, the better informed we are as donors and supporters, as community activists or advocates, the more effective we will become in furthering our particular cause. There are some excellent sources of information on the issues raised in this book. Faith to Action and The Better Care Network both provide online reports and resources that synthesize research findings in this area. Charities like Save the Children publish useful and hard-hitting reports. In the faith sector, groups like ACCI in Australia produce excellent checklists and good practice guidelines for churches and individuals to help them assess and evaluate the sort of initiatives to support. As well as child protection guidelines and financial sustainability, these cover crucial aspects such as proper registration and due process and regulation by the appropriate national authorities.[7] Read reports, ask questions, and probe deeply. If something badges itself as a Christian organization, it doesn't automatically follow that it adheres to the rules nor follows recognized good practice guidelines. Check it out first.

6. Ibid., 5.
7. See ACCI Missions & Relief, *Due Diligence Guidelines*.

Ask the Right Questions

"If you are thinking of supporting an orphanage anywhere in the world, don't even start."[8] This is Caitlin's advice. It may sound terse but it makes the point.

She goes on to say, "Find an alternative. Support a project or initiative that provides prevention, one that strengthens and supports families and the community." There are plenty around. Australian Tara Winkler founded an orphanage in Cambodia and gradually transformed it into an agency that helps vulnerable children escape poverty and be cared for in families. In her book about her experiences, she provides an excellent list of questions to ask before you support a children's organization.[9]

What happens if you are already supporting an orphanage financially? It could be that they are already thinking of or making the transition from a holding home to a family-based care service. Ask them. They need your support. It is scary for any organization to embark on a journey they may not yet fully understand. They'll face new challenges and, of course, may worry what happens to them and their workers. If they aren't at that stage yet, begin the conversation. They do need to start changing focus and again they will require their donors' support. Don't be put off by immediate responses such as, "It won't happen here. The government won't permit it." Dig for answers. Encourage them forward to join the global movement.

Will it affect the children if you withdraw your funds? This is a cause for concern. As governments increasingly fall in line with the UNCRC, then as surely as night follows day, deinstitutionalization is going to be on their agenda. If you support a residential institution, ask them what they are doing to prepare for that process? Suggest they start preparing now. If they don't, someone from the government will come knocking at their door to ask them to conform. Which would they prefer? Start a process intelligently and systematically with professional support? Or turn a blind eye and wait to be called into line or closed down? Talk to SFAC. Talk to one of the other NGOs which specialize in this field. We are here to help.

8. Lance Hope, discussion.

9. Winkler, *How (not)*, 363–65. The questions include the extent to which children are there because of poverty and whether the institution is actively working towards family reunification. Does the organization allow untrained volunteers and visitors to interact with the children without supervision? A child protection policy is ideal but make sure you read it and ensure the organization adheres to it.

Keep It Going

At SFAC we know that quick-fix, knee-jerk solutions tend not to last. By the same token, some programs and initiatives have a natural shelf life. They may do a great deal of good but then it's time to replace them with something else or to wind them down once the objectives are achieved. Tony and Vivienne Hodges say that it's as important to discern when to stop supporting an initiative as to evaluate when to start.[10] Once again, the quality of the relationship is crucial and those of us who run NGOs must never take donors for granted. We owe it to our supporters to keep them informed, consider their opinions, and listen to their feedback. Tony and Vivienne have horror stories of rude and abrupt correspondence from charitable organizations they have supported in the past. Tony says he appreciates that SFAC has never treated him like a human ATM![11] I visit and update the Hodges whenever I can. It's polite, it's the right thing to do, and ensuring a high quality of relationship is the best way to keep supporters engaged. Of course, we are a small NGO. A large organization could not deal with its supporters so individually, but the principle remains the same. It's about relationships, each and every time.

When does it become the right time to cease supporting a project or to wind one down? There is no single answer, of course. Each instance is different but there comes a time when even the best-intentioned initiatives can no longer continue. Brenda and I realized this was the case with the informal residential home run by Pedrinho and Noemi. We supported their work for many years. They were not formally connected to any organization but had simply seen the desperate need and wanted to help. They began by providing hot meals, then a drop-in center which eventually developed into an informal group home of up to forty children.[12] They had no wage and raised funds from donations and charitable events.

Their daughter Mimi stayed with us in Leeds when she came to learn English. She is now married to an Englishman and lives in Manchester. She remembers fun and laughter at the residential home but trauma too. The authorities often arrived at short notice to take younger children to other homes or for adoption. Many of the teenagers stayed for years, until they left school and found work or returned to their families. At one time,

---

10. T. and V. Hodges, discussion.

11. Ibid.

12. Mimi da Silva Lomax, in discussion with Philip Williams, March 28, 2018.

Pedrinho and Noemi had a family of seven in their care. It was highly unlikely anyone would foster or adopt them all! SFAC supported their project financially until it became clear it was unsustainable in the longer term. Nevertheless, the couple had achieved so much and at considerable cost to themselves.

Take Care of Yourself and Others

Mimi was three years old and her brother a toddler when her parents began their work with street children. It felt "normal" to her, the only life she knew. It is only now that she can reflect on how "intense" it all was. Her brother went through a difficult patch, misbehaving at school and clamoring for attention. Mimi believes that it was because of the sheer scale of their extended family. "It was a lovely home but not possible to give everyone the attention they needed." Mimi was exposed to the harsh realities of street life from an early age.

> My parents were very open. They did not hide the background of some of these kids nor what they had been through. After a while I did not want to know any more. It was too traumatic. I saw and heard too much.[13]

When we set out to make a difference, there is always a price to pay. Brenda and I are grateful that we began the journey that led to the formation of SFAC after our boys had grown up. Neither Mark nor Kevin feel that they were in any way disadvantaged by our three years at Bible college, our struggles at Princess Alice Drive, the time we spent in Brazil, or my many trips abroad.[14] Both boys were surprised when we took off for Brazil. Kevin says that he never believed it would happen, particularly not for Brenda. Mark feels that we are both "walking contradictions but not in a bad way." All his life, he had known us to advocate thrift and industry. Take a slow, steady approach. Nothing rash. Learn a trade, earn your crust, don't borrow too much or beyond your means. Then, all of a sudden, we are leaving our jobs and jetting off to Brazil![15] Both sons laugh that I never seem to keep still, I'm either helping Kevin with a boiler or Brenda and I are playing with

13. Ibid.

14. Mark and Kevin Pease, in discussions with Philip Williams, January 24 and May 23, 2018.

15. Mark Pease, discussion.

the grandchildren. As a church leader Mark has seen families damaged when people pursue either business ventures or Christian ministry to the detriment of their family life.[16]

I'll be honest. There have been times when I have missed birthdays and anniversaries. I no longer undertake engagements close to our wedding anniversary. Brenda often jokes about being married to the man who is never there. Dan teases us that she uses my absences as an excuse not to cook but buy a Chinese takeaway meal! For her part, she explains how irritating she finds it when people ask why she doesn't travel with me more often.

"He's at work! It's not a holiday!" Does Joanna, Kevin's wife, accompany him to someone's house when he's fixing a sink or unblocking a pipe with his plumbing business?[17] People have no idea what's involved when you visit a country to assess a program or deliver training. In over thirty visits to Brazil, I have never seen the Amazon rainforest. I've seen tracts of tropical forest so immense that I have some idea what it must be like, but I've never seen it. I would love to see the Amazon, but I am not there to enjoy myself. I am there to work. I am there to make a difference.

There is also the serious issue of personal safety. Brenda suffered tropical illness in Brazil. Caitlin contracted malaria in Africa and Dan postponed proposing to her until she reached the UK. Dan and Walter both laugh about the time when we returned late to a hotel compound in Kampala. The place was locked and there were no lights on. I offered to scale the walls and traverse the compound until I found the security guard who could let us in. I found him alright, aiming at my chest with a bow and seriously sharpened arrow! Some risks are unavoidable and inevitable. Others are easily avoided by proper preparation and planning. You can't avoid risk, but you can minimize the risk to yourself, your organization, and to others. We need to exercise common sense. We need to obey the law and to comply with regulations. If you are running an unlicensed orphanage and reading this, you know what to do!

16. Ibid.

17. Brenda Pease, in discussion with Philip Williams, December 5, 2017.

Keep it Real

"We are dealing with the hardest and harshest things it is ever possible to imagine," says Stephen Servant of Heaven's Family. "We should not sugarcoat or hide that fact."[18]

Let's not kid ourselves. There is nothing appealing or attractive about a teenage street boy. They might be sniffing glue, addicted to drugs. They mug people, attack them in groups. Like Steve Bartel's analogy of the Doberman, you would not want one in your home. Nobody but nobody wants these kids. But they are children. They are human beings.

Everyone responds to pictures of cute and smiling kids. Orphanage tourism thrives on that. Voluntourism thrives on that. At what point does genuine concern topple over into guilt inducement and manipulation? Hug an orphan. Take a selfie. Here are some pictures of smiley toddlers or images of horrific violence. Watch our video. It may shock you into action or it may melt your heart. At SFAC we take great care about the photographs or video footage we present or publish. We don't want to exploit anyone or convey a misleading impression. We are dealing with people's lives. We owe it to them to get things right.

Yes, there is a place for touching images and dramatic accounts. But we must act responsibly. We didn't see the worst Romanian orphanages. At one stage we wondered whether we needed to in order to justify our trips. It was Pete White who pulled us up. "What kind of people are we if we have to see the horror before we respond?" Once the headlines have faded and the media moves on, are we still around to meet the needs that go unnoticed?

Create Ripples

"The thing with our dad is that he just has to be doing something. He won't keep still. When he sees something that needs fixing, he's like a dog with a bone."[19] That is Kevin's assessment! I'm pleased to say, though, that he balances it out by saying, "He's also your best mate. He'll come around to our house and muck in with whatever's going on. They've done what they've done, but they're still my mum and dad and I'm so proud of the pair of them."

18. S. Servant, discussion.
19. Kevin Pease, discussion.

We can only ever be ourselves. I doubt if I'll ever be able to switch off, retire and just play some rounds of golf and forget all about SFAC. But the day will come when I have to let go. I'm confident that I can hand it on in good shape. Dan and Caitlin bring their own particular insights and strengths. Things will develop and evolve, but the core principles will remain the same. Children belong in safe families.

SFAC is appointing new trustees. Among them is Philip Cotterill the retired head of children's services for Kirklees, an adjacent local authority to Leeds City Council. Another is Tory Barrow's husband Glynn Barrow. They have lived in Cambodia doing charity work and are adoptive and foster parents. John Swift, one of our original trustees continues with us, always a go-to guy when I need a sounding board. Everyone at SFAC has appreciated his wise counsel and faithful support. It's great to have him on board as we enter a new phase. John Ellerington has stepped down as a trustee but as a lifelong and faithful friend retains an interest in all we do. We are carrying out project work for well-known global organizations in India, South Africa, and other countries. I recently visited Mexico for the first time. We are producing online training materials and modules. We are adding new projects and new countries to our portfolio.

Whenever we pulled up for the night at a roadside hostel en route to Romania or finished delivering supplies, Pete would use the same laconic phrase, "Job's a good'un!"[20] On one occasion we closed the back of the truck and before Pete could utter his stock phrase, Zolly beat him to it.

"Job's a good'un!" he quipped in his Eastern European accent.

We can all start ripples. We can set them off from right where we are. The job can be a good' un. Your ripples may head off in a different direction from ours. They may be for a different cause entirely. But find one. Find a cause that resonates with you. Ask questions. Investigate it. Learn from those who have gone before you or who are already on the same journey. Start those ripples. Perhaps you'll only hear a light plop in the water, perhaps you'll see the ripples spread out and fade. Perhaps you'll hear a faint echo in the distance. Perhaps you'll see more ripples return.

---

20. Colloquial speech, common in the north of England, meaning the job is all finished satisfactorily.

Epilogue

NIGHT FALLS IN BRAZIL, a brisk tropical dusk. Lights blink on along the rows of bars and smart beachfront hotels. From the awnings of backstreet taverns and street kiosks, improvised strings of lights glow to the pulse and rhythm of the samba. From the favelas and the public parks, the street kids emerge, unseen by day, active at night. Life on the streets is fraught with risks. Few children survive for very long on the streets unless there's some form of intervention. As they make their way through the thick, honking traffic or across vacant lots, other more fortunate children settle down for the night. Most are with their parents or wider families, some in caring homes, others in situations that are less than ideal, but still home, still with family. Others are in children's homes. They may be smaller than they were in the past, but they are still institutions, still not families. A growing number of those without parents or who are unable to stay with their biological families are with guardians or foster families. Some are adopted. The figures are still tiny. Some 932 children were in foster care in the whole of Brazil in 2013. By 2016 that figure was still only 1,837.[1] Nevertheless, they are there, off the streets, out of institutions, with trained and supported foster parents. The Brazilian government set an ambitious target to take all children under the age of six out of residential institutions by 2018. The goal is to place 9,000 children currently in residential care with over 2,000 eligible and professionally assessed Brazilian families through the Família Acolhedora (Family Warmth) scheme. The programs are underway.

I look back on the journey Brenda and I have taken with astonishment and gratitude. Never in our wildest dreams could we have imagined the

1. Brazilian government figures, trans. Delton Hochstedler.

outcomes we have seen. Once we set out, the opportunities came. We didn't go looking for them. Brenda and I often remember the prophecy that the Lord would bring people alongside us. We firmly believe that to be the case. People drew alongside us with help, guidance and support, often in the most unexpected ways. I often quote the scripture, "This is the Lord's doing; it is marvelous in our eyes."[2] I fully believe in providence. If people prefer to put it all down to coincidence and serendipity, let them do so. Either way, it's a remarkable journey and a remarkable story. It's about ordinary people achieving extraordinary things. It's about unlikely people drawn together by a common goal. Ranjit compares it to the way a magnet attracts iron filings. If you put something out there which is right and just and true, people will be drawn toward it, regardless of faith or ideology. The like-minded will work together to bring it about.[3]

In a city apartment, a television glows in the corner. Children cluster to watch or are distracted by the latest games on their cell phones. A teenager prepares to go out. A busy parent takes a moment to check their emails or social media. They may send a message to Mimi, attach a photo of their kids, or tell her about their job. Under gray Manchester skies, Mimi may be transported from the north of England to the vibrancy and color of her native Brazil. She remembers these people from growing up with them in the house they shared with her parents. She remembers the noise and bustle, the joys and the heartaches, the love.

When evening comes in the US or the UK, in Singapore or South Korea, in Australia or New Zealand, someone will sit at a laptop or scroll on their smartphone. There are tweets and blogs and video clips, the noise and clutter of cyberspace. Appeals for funds jostle for attention. It takes just forty seconds to sponsor a child.[4] Click, click, click. Job done, what's next?

How about family-based alternatives? What about the long haul? What funding models best suit such programs and where should the funding go? Is it best deployed to the foster families, to the child's parents, or to the communities themselves? As family-based alternatives to residential care gain traction, there are also implications for government and municipal services. What training and resources are in place? Will programs be

2. Pss 118:23 KJV and NASB.

3. Uppal, discussion.

4. An observation made by Mark Riley, discussion.

funded by the public purse, by private companies, or a combination of the two? What is the role of charities and NGOs?

These are good questions and like the ripples, they continue to spread outward. Start the conversation.

As the sun rises on the African bush, children struggle with cans of water from the riverbanks. Others wake to porridge and fresh water from a JoJo Tank. As dawn breaks across the scarred hills of Myanmar, villagers collect water from an ingenious pipe that snakes up from the spring below. Children stir, from the "source villages" to inner-city Yangon. Some are with their own parents, others with relatives and foster families. The pattern repeats, in Sri Lanka, in Cambodia, in Uganda, in Iraq. The work continues, child by child, case by case, family by family. It involves village elders, grandparents, government, and NGOs. It involves donors, sponsors, social workers, judges, and health professionals. From sunrise to sunset, a movement for social justice grows and spreads. It crosses faiths and creeds, from government departments to voluntary groups, from tiny communities to megacities. It can and should involve us all. Ask yourself, if it were my child or one I care about, a sibling, a cousin, a niece, a nephew, where would I want them to go if they were orphaned or abandoned? Would I want the best for that child or would I simply go along with what others thought should happen? Would I fight for that child's rights, for their voice to be heard and understood? To live in a place that we agree is best and most appropriate? Or would I allow them to be taken away and put in a children's home? If you answer "family" to each question, then let's ensure we give the strongest voice to the children who deserve it most: the vulnerable, lonely, isolated, despised, or rejected. Let's give them the same value we give our own children. You may believe as I do that God sets the lonely in families. You may draw on other ideals and motivations. Surely, we can agree that the most vulnerable children in our world deserve the best not the least. It's time to start building good practice onto good intentions. Children belong in safe families.

Websites

For details about SFAC, see http://sfac.org.uk/.

Readers in the US can also find supporter details at https://globalchildadvocates.org/ and readers in Australia at www.accipartners.org.au/wr166_hope.

NGO websites cited in this book:
ACCI Missions & Relief: https://www.accimissions.org.au/
Action for Children: https://www.actionforchildren.org.uk/
Better Care Network: https://bettercarenetwork.org/
CALM Africa: http://www.calmafrica-ug.org/
Chab Dai: http://chabdai.org/
Children in Families: http://www.childreninfamilies.org/
Formando Vidas: http://colombiastreetkids.org/
Faith to Action Initiative: http://www.faithtoaction.org/
Fundaţia Internaţională pentru Copii, România: https://www.ricf.net/
M'lup Russey: http://mluprussey.org.kh/en/
Rethink Orphanages Network: http://www.rethinkorphanages.org/

Timeline

1948	Brenda Pease (nee Down) is born.
1951	Mick Pease is born.
1966–76	Mick works as coal miner.
1971	Mick and Brenda marry.
1976–79	Birmingham Bible Institute.
1979–82	Houseparents in children's home in the English Midlands.
1982–84	Social work studies at Birmingham Polytechnic.
1984–86	Social worker at NCH children's home in Yorkshire.
1986–2005	Social worker with Leeds City Council specializing in child protection, fostering, and adoption.
1990–93	Four humanitarian visits to Romania.
1994–95	Mick's first visits to Brazil.
1996	Mick's father dies.
1997	Mick and Brenda meet Baroness Cox in Brazil.
1998	Mick returns to Brazil to advocate for foster care.
1999	First visit to Tajikistan.
2000	Mick's mother dies.
2002	Mick establishes SFAC and appoints trustees.
2005	Works part-time for SFAC but continues contract work for Leeds City Council and other agencies until 2015.
2006	Meets Walter Young of Team Fostering in UK; initial training with ABBA in Brazil.

2007	Assists Children in Families in Cambodia.
2009	Brazil passes law to prioritize family-based alternative care.
2010	Works in Myanmar; Mick meets Dan Hope in Leeds.
2012	Visits Paraguay.
2014	Speaks at 3rd International Colloquium on Foster Care in Brazil.
2016	Dan and Caitlin marry.
2017	Mick and Dan address supreme court in Paraguay; Brazilian authorities certify ABBA program. SFAC has worked in over 30 countries and Mick traveled over a million miles.

Bibliography

ACCI Missions & Relief. *Due Diligence Guidelines*. https://d3n8a8pro7vhmx.cloudfront.
   net/acci/pages/145/attachments/original/1505448686/Church-Guide__final_.
   pdf?1505448686.
———. "Kinnected Myanmar—Hani and Thari." Vimeo video, 3:25. Uploaded December
   10, 2017. https://vimeo.com/246707112.
———. *Short-Term Missions and "Orphanages"*. https://d3n8a8pro7vhmx.cloudfront.
   net/acci/pages/145/attachments/original/1505448686/Church-Guide__final_.
   pdf?1505448686.
Australia Government. *Hidden in Plain Sight: An Inquiry into Establishing a Modern Slavery
   Act in Australia*. Canberra: Joint Standing Committee on Foreign Affairs, Defence
   and Trade, 2017. https://www.aph.gov.au/Parliamentary_Business/Committees/
   Joint/Foreign_Affairs_Defence_and_Trade/ModernSlavery/Final_report.
BBC News. "Ethiopia Bans Foreign Adoptions." January 10, 2018. https://www.bbc.co.uk/
   news/world-africa-42635641.
Better Care Network. "Gatekeeping." https://bettercarenetwork.org/library/principles-of-
   good-care-practices/gatekeeping.
Boothby, Neil, et al. "What are the Most Effective Early Response Strategies and
   Interventions to Assess and Address the Immediate Needs of Children Outside of
   Family Care?" *Child Abuse & Neglect* 36 (2012) 711–21.
Bowlby, John. *A Secure Base: Clinical Applications of Attachment Theory*. London:
   Psychology Press, 1988.
Boyd, Andrew. *Baroness Cox: A Voice for the Voiceless*. Oxford: Lion, 1998.
Bunkers, Kelly, et al. *Children, Orphanages, and Families: A Summary of Research to
Help Guide Faith-Based Action*. New York: Faith to Action Initiative/Better Care Network,
   2015.   http://www.faithtoaction.org/wp-content/uploads/2014/03/Faith2Action_
   ResearchGuide_V9_WEB.pdf.
Catholic Relief Services. *American Perceptions of Orphans and Orphanages: An
   Opinion Survey*. Prepared by ORC International, November 2011. http://www.
   changingthewaywecare.org/wp-content/uploads/2017/11/American-Perceptions-
   of-Orphans-and-Orphanages-An-Opinion-Survey-FINAL.pdf.

Cheney, Kristen. "The Orphan Industrial Complex: Charitable Commodification and its Consequences for Child Protection." Prezi slides, uploaded March 2008. http://bit.ly/orphanindustrialcomplex.

Cox, Caroline. *Trajectories of Despair: Misdiagnosis and Maltreatment of Soviet Orphans.* Zurich: Christian Solidarity International, 1991.

Csáky, Corinna. *Keeping Children Out of Harmful Institutions: Why We Should Be Investing in Family-Based Care.* London: Save the Children, 2009. https://www.crin.org/en/docs/Keeping_Children_Out_of_Harmful_Institutions_Final_20.11.09.pdf.

Dahlgreen, Will. "'Brummie' is the least attractive accent." YouGov, December 9, 2014. https://yougov.co.uk/news/2014/12/09/accent-map2/.

De Carvalho, Sarah. *The Street Children of Brazil: One Woman's Remarkable Story.* London: Hodder & Stoughton, 2009.

Doyle, Joanne. *Misguided Kindness: Making the Right Decisions for Children in Emergencies.* London: Save the Children, 2010.

Fahlberg, Vera. *A Child's Journey Through Placement.* London: Jessica Kingsley, 2012.

FICE Youth 2010. *Guidelines for the Alternative Care of Children: A Tool for Reviewing the United Nations Framework with Children—Children's Guide.* 2010. https://bettercarenetwork.org/sites/default/files/Guidelines%20for%20the%20Alternative%20Care%20of%20Children%20-%20A%20Tool%20for%20Reviewing.pdf.

Foley, Erin. "From Lonely Orphan to Loved Son." June 21, 2016. https://www.childreninfamilies.org/from-lonely-orphan-to-loved-son/.

Gale, Chrissie, and Corinna Csáky. *Making Decisions for the Better Care of Children: The Role of Gatekeeping in Strengthening Family-based Care and Reforming Alternative Care Systems.* [New York?]: UNICEF/Better Care Network, 2015. https://bettercarenetwork.org/library/principles-of-good-care-practices/gatekeeping/making-decisions-for-the-better-care-of-children-the-role-of-gatekeeping-in-strengthening-family.

Gilbert, Lela. *Baroness Cox: Eyewitness to a Broken World.* Oxford: Monarch, 2007.

Gray, Philip H. "Henry Dwight Chapin: Pioneer in the study of institutionalized infants." *Bulletin of the Psychonomic Society* 27.1 (1989) 85–87.

Greenfield, Craig. *The Urban Halo: A Story of Hope for Orphans of the Poor.* London: Authentic Media, 2007.

Hague Conference on Private International Law. Hague Convention on Protection of Children and Co-operation in Respect of Intercountry Adoption. May 29, 1993. https://www.hcch.net/en/instruments/conventions/full-text/?cid=69.

————. *The Implementation and Operation of the 1993 Hague Intercountry Adoption Convention: Guide to Good Practice: Guide No 1 under the Hague Convention of 29 May 1993 on Protection of Children and Co-operation in Respect of Intercountry Adoption.* Bristol: Family Law, 2008. https://assets.hcch.net/upload/adoguide_e.pdf.

Higginbotham, Peter. "Introduction." http://www.workhouses.org.uk/intro/.

————. "Princess Alice Orphanage, Sutton Coldfield, Warwickshire." http://www.childrenshomes.org.uk/SuttonColdfieldNCH/.

IRIN News, "Protecting Children from Orphan-Dealers." May 27, 2009. http://www.irinnews.org/report/84582/west-africa-protecting-children-orphan-dealers.

Joyce, Kathryn. *Child Catchers: Rescue, Trafficking, and the New Gospel of Adoption.* New York: Public Affairs, 2013.

———. "The Trouble with the Christian Adoption Movement." *New Republic*, January 11, 2016. https://newrepublic.com/article/127311/trouble-christian-adoption-movement.

Karim, Shaykh Zuber. *Adoption and Fostering in the UK: Islamic Guidance on the Contemporary Practice of Adoption and Fostering in the UK*. Wakefield: Penny Appeal, 2018.

Kaye, Randi, and Wayne Drash. "Kids for Sale: 'My Mom was Tricked.'" CNN, October 14, 2017. https://edition.cnn.com/2017/10/12/health/uganda-adoptions-investigation-ac360/index.html.

Knaus, Christopher. "Orphanage tourism a 'scam' fostered by Australians, Liberal senator says." *Guardian*, April 17, 2018. https://www.theguardian.com/world/2018/apr/17/orphanage-tourism-a-scam-fostered-by-australians-liberal-senator-says.

Llorente, María Ángeles García, et al., *Children in Institutions: The Beginning of the End?* Florence: UNICEF, 2003.

Lumos Foundation. "Children in Orphanages: A Hidden Global Problem." February 24, 2017. https://www.wearelumos.org/resources/children-orphanages-hidden-global-problem/.

Marshall, Katherine. "Need Plus Greed." OnFaith, August 31, 2009. https://www.onfaith.co/onfaith/2009/08/31/need-plus-greed/2295.

Martin, T. Hartley. "Treatment of the Tuberculous Cripple at the Hospital for Children, Leasowe," *British Medical Journal* (November 1919): 664.

Morris, Tina, and Jonathon Priestley, eds. *Journeys of Hope: 12 Lives Changed by God*. Bradford: Christians Against Poverty Books, 2008.

Narey, Martin, and Mark Owers. *Foster Care in England*. London: Department for Education, 2018.

Nelson, Charles, Nathan Fox, Charles Zeanah, and Dana Johnson (Bucharest Early Intervention Project). "Caring for Orphaned, Abandoned and Maltreated Children." PowerPoint slides. Child Rights International Network online, 2007. https://www.crin.org/en/docs/PPT%20BEIP%20Group.pdf.

New Horizon. "History." https://newhorizon.org.uk/about/history-in-summary/.

Petrowski, Nicole, Claudia Cappa, and Peter Gross. "Estimating the Number of Children in Formal Alternative Care: Challenges and Results." *Child Abuse & Neglect* 70 (2017): 288–398.

Pinheiro, Paulo Sérgio. *World Report on Violence Against Children*. Geneva: United Nations, 2006. https://www.unicef.org/violencestudy/reports.html.

Powell, G., T. Chinake, D. Mudzinge, W. Maambira, and S. Mukutiri. *Children in Residential Care: The Zimbabwean Experience*. Harare: Ministry of Public Service, Labour and Social Welfare of Zimbabwe/UNICEF, 2004. https://bettercarenetwork.org/library/the-continuum-of-care/residential-care/children-in-residential-care-the-zimbabwean-experience.

Qui, Linda. "J.K. Rowling's Charity Wants to End Orphanages. Here's Why." Politifact, January 4, 2017. http://www.politifact.com/global-news/statements/2017/jan/04/lumos/jk-rowlings-charity-wants-end-orphanages-heres-why/.

Riley, Mark. "Volunteers are Fueling the Growth of Orphanages in Uganda. They need to stop." *Guardian*, May 16, 2016. https://www.theguardian.com/global-development-professionals-network/2016/may/16/volunteers-stop-visiting-orphanages-start-preserving-families.

———. "Uganda's Official Alternative Care Framework: Situation Analysis and Response." Presentation at the Children without Appropriate Care in Uganda Workshop, Kampala, Uganda, December 4, 2013.

Ucembe, Stephen. "My Experience of Volunteers: Growing up in an 'Orphanage' in Kenya." http://www.rethinkorphanages.org/growingupinanorphanage/.

UK Government. *Children Looked After in England (Including Adoption), Year Ending 31 March 2017*. SFR 50/2017, September 28, 2017. London: Department for Education, 2017.

———. "Children's Social Care Data in England 2017: Main Findings." August 31, 2017. https://www.gov.uk/government/publications/childrens-social-care-data-in-england-2017/childrens-social-care-data-in-england-2017-main-findings.

———. "Types of Honours and Awards." https://www.gov.uk/honours/types-of-honours-and-awards.

UNICEF. "Orphans." https://www.unicef.org/media/media_45279.html.

United Nations Convention on the Rights of the Child (UNCRC). New York, November 20, 1989, 1577 U.N.T.S. https://treaties.un.org/doc/Treaties/1990/09/19900902%20 03–14%20AM/Ch_IV_11p.pdf.

United Nations General Assembly. Resolution 64/142, "Guidelines for the Alternative Care of Children." February 24, 2010. https://www.unicef.org/protection/alternative_care_Guidelines-English.pdf.

Whetton, Kathryn, et al. "Three-Year Change in the Wellbeing of Orphaned and Separated Children in Institutional and Family-Based Care Settings in Five Low- and Middle-Income Countries." *PLOS ONE* 9.8 (2014). https://doi.org/10.1371/journal.pone.0104872.

Williams, Andrew. *Working with Street Children: An Approach Explored*. London: Russell House, 2011.

Williamson, John, and Aaron Greenberg. *Families, Not Orphanages*. New York: Better Care Network, 2010. https://bettercarenetwork.org/library/particular-threats-to-childrens-care-and-protection/effects-of-institutional-care/families-not-orphanages.

Winkler, Tara. *How (Not) to Start an Orphanage . . . By a Woman Who Did*. Sydney: Allen & Unwin, 2016.

Lightning Source UK Ltd.
Milton Keynes UK
UKHW022058260819
348645UK00011B/235/P